RESONANCE

Resonance

RESONANCE

NINE PRACTICES

FOR

HARMONIOUS
HEALTH

AND

VITALITY

JOYCE WHITELEY HAWKES, PH.D.

HAY HOUSE, INC.

Carlsbad, California • New York City
London • Sydney • Johannesburg
Vancouver • Hong Kong • New Delhi

Published and distributed in the United States by: Hay House, Inc.

Design: Pam Homan

Photos: Fax Sinclair (www.fax-sinclair.com, *Attention and Focus, Resonance and Transformation*), Helen Folsom *(Balance and Harmony)*, and Joyce Whiteley Hawkes

The information contained in this book is not intended to diagnose, treat, prevent, or cure any disease, or to provide specific medical advice. Questions about the relationship between nutrition, supplements, meditative practices and your health should be directed to a qualified health practitioner. The reader and associated health professionals are responsible for evaluating the risks of any therapy reviewed in this book. Those responsible made every effort possible to thoroughly research the accuracy of the information and assume no responsibility for errors, inaccuracies, or omissions.

Hardcover ISBN: 978-1-4019-2908-4

Printed in the United States of America

To my beloved teacher and master healer,
Jero Mangku Srikandi

CONTENTS

INTRODUCTION

Being human is a strange and wonderful experience. We are big enough to fall like Newton's apple, yet our cells are small enough and work fast enough to qualify our inner workings as a quantum universe. We inhabit a borderland between Newtonian physics and the quantum model of reality, and we smoothly operate within these two realities. The body handles the details of the intricate workings of our 100 trillion cells without our conscious intervention. When we consider our spiritual nature, we encounter another borderland. The closer we come to an experience of oneness, or union, in the classic spiritual sense, the more our personal reality merges with the Divine—existing in an embrace at the threshold between flesh and spirit.

Each chapter of this book presents two aspects of our human nature that invoke and deepen the interfaces within us. The energies of the two thresholds resonate. Indeed, the whole universe exists in harmonic resonance. Atoms vibrate and their complex arrays of matter, from mountains to moons to mothers, move with those vibrations. The nine couplet practices in this book help us access some aspects of that universal resonance for ourselves. Although there are many more components to our innate nature, these nine practices enable you to enter the dance of harmony, find healing, and discover renewed vitality.

In that regard, each chapter title reflects a quality that resides naturally in us. These word pairs are intended to invoke, expand, and provide access to those qualities in a new way. The science in this book illustrates the interface where spirit and body meet, and there is mystery at many of those edges where knowledge reaches its current limits. Although there is an intuitively resonant meaning in each couplet, the experience of the universal qualities of each can deepen for you through practice. Think of this book as a guide to assist your exploration of nine practical approaches to health and nine practices that hold the potential for expanded awareness of your own healing nature. All the practices can be applied to self-healing and to assisting others.

Sooner or later we all face challenges with these biological, Newtonian bodies we have. Illness or injury may stop us in our tracks. Resonance becomes dissonance, leaving us to wonder what to do, where to find help, and why we are in such a state. In my work over the past four decades, I have asked these questions in the fields of science and spirituality—of indigenous healers in other parts of the world, colleagues, physicians, academics, and thousands of clients, for whom I have been a direct facilitator of healing. Out of that learning, these nine paired principles emerge as guideposts to support our health. Each set of pairs highlights skills that our healing nature can develop. Likewise, each chapter includes stories that illustrate the practical application of the couplets. Simple practices conclude each chapter and give us access to both worlds: our biology and our spirituality. These practices offer you the means to train yourself in states of consciousness that support robust health and provide a healing path when illness arises.

Resonance provides ways of knowing and living in our often puzzling world where we dance between the analytical, logical, data-driven concepts and the flashes of intuition, insight, and the unexpected. Both analysis and intuition can be effective companions, if not friends. I entered my personal dance far on the side of the analytical and data-based world of biophysics as a research scientist discovering secrets of the body's cells. My highly sophisticated tools included electron microscopes, X-ray microanalysis, and Q-switched rapid-pulse lasers. Following a near-death experience I was plunged into the consciousness of the intuitive. Changes to how I lived and what I did with the gifts I discovered did not come all at once. At first I relied upon my familiar way of making decisions with strong focus and analysis. In more relaxed moments, I noticed that an intuitive idea would pop into my consciousness and those ideas were both useful and appropriate. These handy intuitive pops did not happen every time I needed to make a decision, however, and I learned that I could use all the skills of my mind. With time, the tools of analytical practice and intuitive practice ceased to be in conflict for me, and my life became a joyful dance that honored both.

During decades of use and refinement of these tools as a scientist and healing facilitator, I faced many challenges and struggled with a steep learning curve. Early in my quest, I took my questions to highly competent individuals in the United States, the Philippines, India, England, and Bali. They, too, understood the dance between logic and intuition, between states of consciousness in the ordinary world and in the expanded reality of spiritual experience.

Ultimately we can learn to walk a middle way—the edge of the interface of both—with delight, healing, and curiosity. Each day is a new journey on that edge and cannot be second-guessed. A renewed sense of wonder returns again and again, as we live a practical life in the luminosity of expanded awareness.

In today's world, the science of neurophysiology—how our neurons affect our body's function—is one of the most strongly advancing fields of research. Every time new technology, such as the functional MRI, is developed, new insights are gained into the science of how the body and brain function. Until just a few years ago, the brain was considered a linear structure in which one neuron connected to another and that one to another. It was believed that thoughts and sensory input proceeded in a neat sequence. But under the closer scrutiny made possible by advances in medical technology, that hypothesis didn't hold up. Indeed, we know now, from scanning images of the brain at work, that neuronal activity lights up in numerous parts of the brain simultaneously when we are thinking or when our sensory systems are stimulated. Our skulls contain a self-organizing processor that is more than a wonder—the brain is utterly magnificent.

Once discounted as the placebo effect (a health benefit brought about by the expectation of improvement or the faith of the patient in the treatment), the study of complementary and alternative medicine is a field yielding new, sound scientific advances. Research findings have dispelled the idea that the placebo effect isn't "real," focusing instead on learning more about the complex mechanisms by which the activity of the mind brings about very real changes in the brain and the body. The National Institutes of Health now fund large studies to identify more clearly the effectiveness of biologically based practices, energy medicine, manipulative body-based techniques, and mind-body techniques. Some 40 percent of Americans use the above modalities to supplement their health care.[1]

Additionally, recent advancement in the science of brain function has shown that the two halves of the brain are intimately connected. We do not run our lives predominately on one side or the other. Indeed, the brain continually coordinates all aspects of function through pathways previously unappreciated. Some of those pathways, curiously enough, are mediated by specific cells called astrocytes, or star cells. Our brains are exquisitely synchronized and interconnected.

My work has spanned nearly 40 years, half of them in solid scientific research in cellular biology and half in the practice of energy medicine and healing practices, many of them grounded in indigenous healing traditions. Although I left my position as head of an electron microscopy laboratory in 1984, it was several years before I embarked on the first trip to the Philippines to study with a healer for three months. In 1990, I traveled to Bali and met my first teacher, Jero Tapakan. Subsequently, I returned many times over a ten-year period and worked exclusively with Jero Mangku Srikandi. I am grateful to the teachers who have shared their journeys and profound wisdom with me.

This book incorporates stories from the field, from direct experience with these healers, and from the ever-expanding world of cutting-edge cell research. Within this book, I offer you healing practices that resonate with science and spirit. You will find informative summaries and fascinating scientific findings from the current research into cell "language," including cell signaling and cell communication. Against this biological backdrop, you'll find mind-body practices: imagery, insight, and empowering healing practices. The outcome is healing that bridges the gap between the biology of cells and the mystery of human existence.

It is important to acknowledge that there is a gap in the scientific understanding of the mechanisms through which energy medicine works. I will not attempt to create a cosmology or theoretical explanation that fills that gap. As a scientist, I know the connections are not yet clear, but as a healer, I know with certainty that the connections are there. And those who experience healing are confident that their health has improved with the application of these practices. Despite the gap in understanding, there is sturdy ground on which to advance our knowledge, understanding, and practical applications of cell-level healing.

I encourage you to engage your own healing practice from a place that feels comfortable or familiar for you— one that is a natural extension of your own history and your own sensibilities. Perhaps for you that begins with a strong relationship with nature or a spiritual or religious tradition that informs your life. Perhaps illness, adversity, or a sense of powerlessness has become a defining context for your life and you seek sturdier inner ground on which to build health and hope. This book is about going deeper in your own spiritual practice to become an exceptional healer for yourself or potentially for others.

I encourage you to use this book as a guide to open gateways of personal experience.
I encourage you to explore for yourself.
I encourage you to trust yourself.

CHAPTER 1

APPRECIATION AND AWARENESS

I have inside me the winds, the deserts, the oceans, the stars, and everything created in the universe.

— PAULO COELHO

I don't exactly recall what was on my list of things to do that day in December 1976, but certainly death was not one of them. I was the head of a research laboratory in Seattle, Washington, where we used electron microscopes to study the effects of pollutants on fish. The lab was with the National Marine Fisheries Service, a branch of the National Oceanic and Atmospheric Administration. Our facility sat on the edge of a ship canal that connected two huge lakes, part of the watery charm of Seattle. With five assistants, two electron microscopes, a state-of-the-art photographic darkroom, and all kinds of fancy equipment

1

to do our work, we were a busy research group: publishing papers and traveling in the United States and abroad to talk to groups of scientists. It was a time of excitement and career success for me. I had won the respect of my colleagues for earlier work with a high-speed ruby laser and its biological effects, and enjoyed the elected position of fellow with the American Association for Advancement of Science. I loved every minute of this work.

I did not spend much time at home, nor did I love housework. On a Friday night I was hurriedly cleaning house and had no idea that in minutes my life would change abruptly. The vacuum cleaner chugged along with me through the bedroom, down the long hallway, and I had nearly finished the living room. The last sweep was in front of the fireplace hearth, 15 inches away from the mantel. I did not bump the mantel or touch the fireplace, yet in a flash a heavy, leaded-glass art piece framed in thick oak toppled off the mantel onto my head. I crumpled to the carpet, crushing pain shot through my head, and I was out. From there on nothing was ordinary. My awareness no longer resided in my body. I had no sense of a body, or of my house, or of living across the street from Greenlake in Seattle, or even of my own name.

I was zipping along a long, dark tunnel, drawn to a beautiful and welcoming light far ahead. At the end of this tunnel, just before the entrance to the lighted place, my deceased mother and grandmother stood. They were radiant with good health, glowing with love, and welcomed me wordlessly. I was overwhelmed to see them. I had missed them intensely, but had no belief in an afterlife, so seeing them astonished me. It seemed like we were together for an eternity, and yet I moved on without remorse or sadness into the place where the light was stronger still.

I marveled at the beauty of the scene before me. The sky was a shade of blue that I had only seen in the high mountains just before dusk—almost iridescent—with a richness never seen in cities. The luminous color lifted my spirit. The hues did not fade as if night were approaching but stayed glowing with awe-inspiring brightness. The surroundings were suffused with light. I seemed to be standing on a slight rise with a sweeping view of rolling hills. The colors reached out with brilliance. Blades of grass glowed with a quality of green that sparkled without a hint of harshness. The flowers glowed as if each petal and leaf emitted its own light. My being was immersed in peace and tranquility. I had a relaxed inner hum of joy and such fullness of awareness that to leave or anticipate leaving was unthinkable. I was fully present in a manner that I had never experienced before. I walked down the hillock into a bit of a valley while I continued in the fullness of each moment. There was no sense of the passage of time or concern about what time it was or if there was anything else at all to do except to be fully present. What an unexpected surprise that this glorious place could be my destination: I was a staunch atheist. I had never heard of near-death experiences and had no inkling about spiritual experience in expanded realities.

Before I could think much more about how this all happened and without a forewarning of the impending change, I found myself transported to another location. I saw steps and a platform that softly glowed with a golden light. I was drawn to walk up the steps onto the platform toward the one and only being I saw. No voice told me to do that and no mind chatter argued whether I should or should not approach the being. Some feeling of welcome, safety, and joy drew me up the steps without hesitation.

Light infused everything. I felt buoyant and totally at peace. The same sense of each moment having its own relaxed fullness was there as it was in the place of rolling hills. I had no desire to leave, no desire to be or do anything other than bask in the luminous presence before me and all around me. There was no fear in me and no anticipation whatsoever.

At some point in this reverie I recognized that my entire life was fully known and each part of it was understood and not judged. Did this awareness come from outside of me or well up from inside? I could not tell, but it gave me freedom from self-judgment. Suddenly I was abruptly back on the floor of my living room with an excruciatingly sore head. I reached my hand to the hurt place and found a mat of dried blood. I was shocked to realize that I had been out for more than a few seconds. How long had I been unconscious? It was—maybe more. I did not seek medical help until Monday morning when my co-workers whisked me off to a doctor, who found a blood clot on my brain. I was instructed to go home and rest for a few weeks, but I did not need surgery. I had always been so healthy and physically active as a skier, mountain climber, and hiker that this was a major change for me.

I was flooded with new appreciation for my life. I was equally flooded with new awareness of the expanse of possible realities. To be sure, as my awareness of the certainty of an afterlife expanded so did my appreciation of the precious moments of human existence. Initially, I tried to dismiss the entire vision of "the other side," but I could not shake the impact of the peace, joy, and clarity I felt. The images were brilliantly fixed in my mind.

Fortunately, my recovery was complete with no functional or clinical brain damage. I returned to the lab and the work there, but I also began searching for books and people who knew about near-death experience. I found a local healer and took classes with him. I began meditating daily. Some seven years later, and after a profound visionary calling to healing, I resigned my position at the laboratory and opened a small office as a healing facilitator. Now, 26 years later, these decades of work, meditation, travel, and writing continue full of joy, growth, new insights, and great appreciation for all that has happened.

Recently, I was swapping stories of near-death experiences with a fellow in a neighborhood coffee shop. He had passed out from a drug overdose and was taken to a hospital. At the time, he had no belief in spirituality and no belief in God. He recalls how he floated above his body and looked down on himself on a surgical table. He heard a doctor say that they were losing him. Then he zoomed back toward his body and remembers nothing after that. Years and years later after his recovery, he continues to wonder what aspect of his mind or spirit might exist beyond the biology of his brain. What could produce such an image, such an episode? He said that the event is as fresh today as when it happened 25 years ago. As he told me about it, shivers ran up and down my spine. In turn, I related my experience to him; the images I saw and feelings I had were also as fresh as if they happened a day—rather than decades—ago.

Our perception is remarkably variable. We have a choice to either keep a narrow outlook or to relax and open to an expansive view. Fortunately, it does not take a near-death experience to increase awareness nor to embrace a fuller appreciation of life. In my case, as a thoroughly hard-headed person, I've often thought that it *did* take a crack on the head to get my attention. Now I listen more easily and quickly, not out of fear of another injury, but from a place of remembering the exquisiteness of the other side, and how I felt totally known and loved. My understanding of reality changed permanently. If we are touched by the divine presence during meditation, in synagogue, in a mosque, in church, in the wilderness, or wherever it may happen, the result can bring new insights. How we see our lives and the world around us is transformed.

Awareness draws us once again to notice what dimension of reality we have engaged. In everyday experience we know that several dimensions of reality impinge on us constantly whether we are aware of them or not. The pull of gravity keeps our feet on the planet while the mystery of the dark matter and dark energy of the universe penetrates every aspect of our inner and outer lives. We cannot describe or discern the impact of what can neither be seen nor measured. Existing outside of the electromagnetic spectrum this unknown stuff is a huge part of us, everything around us, and everything far away from our planet. If we zoomed into space and traveled to the Orion nebula, 1,500 light-years away, we could witness the destruction of old stars. We would see the efficacy of the universe in recycling all matter in the dynamic process of reworking the aged star stuff. The birth of new stars would happen before our eyes from that very material. Along with what we see through telescopes, the secret work of dark matter and energy mixes its influence into the wonder of star birth.

Intentional Shifts That Expand Awareness

When we remove the restrictions of limited perception, life opens up in ordinary and extraordinary ways. There is a quality of gratitude that can shift awareness in the hubbub and the crush of ordinary activities—the morning routine, the sameness of going to work, paying bills, and cleaning the kitchen. A friend of mine, Hilde, an exceedingly successful small-business owner, scolded me when I whined about the time it took to write checks for bills. I expressed how I despised doing that chore from the aspect of both time and the resulting reduction in my bank balance. She explained her way of paying bills. Hilde developed a practice in which she lit a candle or two, played music she loved, and blessed each and every check she wrote. She noticed that business improved not just a bit, but in a significant way when she carried out this ritual. The improvement was consistent and dropped off when she was rushed and did not spend time with specific appreciation for the resources to pay the utilities, the rent, and all those other fundamental business expenses. Her blessing was one of gratitude for the funds to pay the bills and gratitude for work that brought in sufficient money to keep her business robust. Her massage practice grew into the most highly respected massage school in the area.

TUNE IN TO RESONANCE

The next time you need to pay your bills, take a moment to sit down. Try Hilde's approach: Create a comfortable space at your desk or tabletop that is dedicated to the task. Include a candle, a small vase with a flower, and a bowl of your favorite cookies (or sliced apples, pecans, or any sweet treat you enjoy). As you pick up each invoice or statement, take a moment to actively appreciate the service that was provided and your ability to pay the required money. As you seal the envelope, bless the transaction. If you pay bills online, you can modify the space to include your computer. The same kind of appreciation can be generated as you click the mouse to send the money electronically.

In a spiritual healing practice, we may hope for an instantaneous miracle yet never know exactly how the healing will manifest itself in the dimensions of time and space. One client, Ellen, came to me with a severe eye problem. Her ophthalmologist could do no more for her and warned her about impending blindness. Her right eye was worse than the left one. She showed me the extent of the problem by filling in black shading on a grid that represented her field of vision. Three quarters of her visual field was in total darkness. In our first session, Ellen described the lack of color and the lack of definition in that right eye. She could see a bit of light and a lot of dark. Her left eye also had a good-sized region of darkness, but the center of her field of vision was colorful and clear. Together we held the intention for her eyes to heal physically. This was Ellen's first experience with energy healing, and she was fully engaged in the process, though she had a healthy skepticism about whether it would work or not, given the dire diagnosis of her physician. Her retina was bumpy—attached at certain places and puffed out at other locations. When Ellen got up at the end of the session, she squinted one eye and then the other and with disappointment in her voice said that she could detect no difference. I encouraged her to give the work a few days to bring about noticeable change. The body takes some time—biological time—to heal. Miracles are wonderful, of course, and do happen, but healing may also occur at a slower pace.

She called me after three days, so excited. The vision in her right eye was appreciably better. As we worked every few weeks, she regained more and more sight. She could see colors, and images were visible in the right eye where only an undifferentiated light and dark had been seen before. Over a number of months of work, she regained much of her sight in both eyes. During this time, she had a few setbacks when the image was less clear and more darkness covered the field. Each time, however, we've been able to open the expanse of what she can see. Although not perfect, her eyesight is so much better that her quality of life has improved dramatically. She can drive, read, and move confidently in the world.

Progress in this case has been slow and steady, not instantaneous, yet wonderfully gratifying. For Ellen, the results of intentionally focused healing sessions changed her physical awareness. Her internal and spiritual awareness changed, too. As her eyes improved, the direct experience of healing became part of her reality. It was easier and easier for her to bring a quality of appreciation to each day. As appreciation increased, fear decreased, and that made healing more accessible. Fear seems to set up a barrier that prevents the flow of healing to get close enough to touch us.

Unexpected Shifts That Expand Awareness

He sat with his legs crossed, back straight, and head tilted ever so slightly forward. Breath by breath his mind became calm, settled, and quieted. As in every other practice, Rick, a friend of mine, anticipated that a quiet comfort would develop as the minutes ticked away. Without prelude and without foreknowledge of the possibility of such phenomena, Rick's inner visual field filled with bright light—an intensely glowing purple with overtones of the deepest red. At first, the images intrigued him from the aspect of a visual oddity as they swirled and shifted from one design to another. Once the novelty wore off, Rick also noticed a flow of energy throughout his body. From the top of his head down through his chest, abdomen, legs, and feet, the flow was perceptible. The pain in his back subsided. His worries about whether the neighbors would build a garage that blocked his view vanished. A distinct but soft presence of peace settled into his mind. His perception of time shifted into timelessness. If he sat for 3 minutes or 300 minutes made no difference to his state of mind. As Rick returned to ordinary consciousness, he was aware of how good he felt physically and mentally, and how he had been open to a spiritual blessing but never anticipated such an extraordinary event. He wanted to experience the colors again, but could not make them happen no matter how hard he scrunched his brow, repeated mantras, or applied any other desire-driven technique. What he discovered was that sitting for meditation with no agenda other than the simplest connection with spirit was often accompanied by some sort of vibrant light show. Each time there were different colors, designs, and durations. Each time the sense of blessing deepened, and he returned to his daily activities with a resonance of compassion for himself and all whom he encountered.

Many of us have a belief that we must work hard at goodness to be blessed. We seek to find a particular path in life, a vocation, a reason for being. We are convinced that the pursuit of that path has one outcome, which will give us joyous days, nights, and years. For unanticipated grace to bless us for no particular reason is outside the paradigm of that belief. From just such remarkable occurrences as Rick's we might come to a different conclusion. Perhaps we are here basically to discover who we are and that we can connect with the source of the universe. Any particular path of service would flow naturally from our unique skills and gifts. The one path becomes a path of being rather than specific activity. Destiny is seen as connection and blessing.

TUNE IN TO RESONANCE

Envision a path in front of you that represents your deepest sense of how you would like your journey through life to appear. Do you see a shaded glen with sounds of a flowing stream, a forested trail fragrant with cedar, a meadow scented with wildflowers, or . . . ? Look to where you have come from on the path, where you are now, and where you are headed. Bless every step you have taken and will take, then come fully to the place and moment of now. You have set many things in motion in your life; and they inform you about your impact on others, your skills, and your happiest and most challenged times. Underneath it all is a self that has integrity and worthiness. Appreciate the truest sense of the being that you are, and enjoy the path of connection without demands for performance. Dance in the light of presence as you trust yourself to naturally express your gifts and abilities.

There are times when any one of us may be headed in a direction that makes perfect sense and seems to be exactly right. Major or minor course corrections can move the route into unknown territory and unanticipated outcomes. An attitude of appreciation for each surprise step and intersection is useful.

A man in his 30s came to me as a client. He had lived a rough life before he walked through my office door. Diagnosed with schizophrenia, Mike had attempted suicide by swallowing a huge number of pills. If that wasn't hard enough on his digestive system, the stomach pump in the ER, charcoal, and other treatments had left him with severe stomach cramps and diarrhea. Those symptoms continued for well over a year after the attempt, and these were his main healing concerns when he came in for his first session with me. The focus of healing was to support his body to repair severely damaged cells of the stomach and intestinal lining. Both columnar surface cells and mucosal cells were included. The microscopic fingers of the absorptive surface of the intestines, the microvilli, had been damaged and could not function well enough to transport nutrients into his bloodstream.

Mike's body responded quickly to our work evidenced by a reduction in the severity and frequency of his diarrhea. After some months with sessions every other week, his digestive system had settled to a reasonably normal and steady state. I was startled when he said, "How about we work on my schizophrenia?" We made some firm agreements. He would not change his medications without the knowledge and consent of his psychiatrist, and he would also continue regular psychiatric appointments.

Part of each session with me included an assessment of how he felt and what symptoms he had. One that distressed him had happened several years prior to our work. He was experiencing sensations of something touching him and moving physically. On one occasion that tactile hallucination shoved him into a busy street and pushed him to sit down in the middle of rush-hour traffic. How he survived that episode without being struck by a car was itself a miracle.

To enter into healing work for Mike's schizophrenia and particularly the tactile hallucinations was new for me. In this situation, I spent considerable time in meditation before our sessions, and in consultation with his psychiatrist, and I reviewed the literature on brain structure.

During our one-on-one sessions, I allowed the background material to be just that—background—and relied on the guidance that came spiritually. The first part of each session included work to clear energy blockages and to support the natural flow of energy through his body. The sensation of an easy movement of energy came to my hands as I moved them about eight inches above Mike's body. For him, the sensation was of deep relaxation and an emotional sense of peace. In the second part of the session I let myself go into a deep silence. As I waited in that state, guidance would come to me on how to proceed. The confluence of what I had studied and a euphoric lightness merged as I felt energy move through me to Mike. The energy was focused on his brain and moved within its different parts as the session proceeded. His experience, as we debriefed after the session, was of being relaxed in a way that was peaceful, safe, and on the verge of sleep. It was not always easy for him to pop right out of that state at the end of the session. It felt so good; he was reluctant to return from that place. It took some minutes for him to reorient to the ordinary world.

In just three sessions, his primary symptom—the tactile hallucination of being touched when no one was there—progressively lessened. I encouraged Mike to establish a practice of appreciation and finish every day with gratitude for the positive changes he experienced. Each appointment revealed new levels of healing. His psychiatrist encouraged him to reduce the dosage of his medication, eventually to needing no medication. Mike's quality of life improved dramatically. He went back to school, got an excellent job, purchased a car, and left public assistance and public housing. His psychiatrist told him that he is among only one percent of people with his diagnosis who are able to so extensively transform their lives. In cases such as these, appreciation comes naturally, and the awareness of the possibility of healing such an intense disability stretches the boundaries of conventional wisdom. Not an instantaneous miracle, but a progressive miracle—Mike changed his health and healed his life.

The Science of Awareness: What Inhibits, What Helps

We know that stress is a problem. It shoves us out of resonance. How that occurs biologically is quite revealing. Cortisol, which is produced by the adrenal glands during stress, has a number of actions. One of those is to attack the myelin sheath that encircles nerve fibers. When a nerve cell loses its myelin, it cannot transmit signals. No transmission—no awareness. Long-term stress causes death of nerve cells and that includes the neurons of the brain. Awareness is not totally a function of how many neurons are at work, but the fewer brain cells, the less opportunity for adequate cognitive function. Not that many years ago the loss of brain cells was considered to be permanent. Current research shows that neurons do divide and make new cells. The surprise is what promotes the production of these new cells—neurogenesis in the brain. Studies supported by the National Institutes of Health and picked up by the popular press have shown that blueberries and Sudoku are not the panacea they were once thought to be.[1] Three activities, however, have been identified that do help our brains make new neurons and improve the synapses or connections between nerve cells. Those connections form circuits that involve numerous neurons. Extensive circuits of various lengths increase cognitive function that enables us to develop skills and to remember many aspects of a particular activity or series of thoughts needed to make a decision.

What does help the brain and its cells function optimally? Exercise, meditation, and fine motor skills that develop with certain video and computer games have all proven to promote brain power. Exercise is the number-one activity that promotes the formation of new connections in the brain. Data from Art Kramer of the University of Illinois at Urbana-Champaign says that "a year of exercise can give a 70-year-old the connectivity of a 30-year-old, improving memory, planning, dealing with ambiguity, and multitasking." Exercise appears to enhance the cell-level requirements for superior cognition. The molecular needs of brain cells to function and to transmit their messages to the proper circuit of cells directly benefit from exercise. The capacity of neurons to connect with each other in a network is mind-boggling. In fact, the human brain with its 100 billion neurons, a huge population to begin with, can make 100 trillion connections.[2] When billions of cells make trillions of connections they form a high level of complexity. The more cellular connections, the smarter we are. More awesome even than the massive numbers of neurons and connections are the ways they reliably function to move muscles, create thoughts, compose music, and write words.

TUNE IN TO RESONANCE

Take a moment of appreciation for the way your brain works, for its complexity, and for its ability to make the network of connections that enable your perception, your activity, and your judgment. Think of some of the specifics of how your body works without your attention: blood cells flow through your veins, intestinal cells replenish without conscious thought.

You breathe without having to remember to inhale. Then there are your own abilities to master difficult tasks, make healthy lifestyle choices, or generally manage the complexities of modern life. Allow appreciation to build in your mind and subsequently create awareness of the blessings that abide with you. Enjoy these combined qualities long enough for the emotions of wonder and awe to develop.

Studies on one brain region, the visual cortex, indicate that it is not the genetic codes that create this complexity, but the self-organizing ability of the brain cells that craft the networks of complex connections.[3] Exactly how a self-organized system accomplishes such a feat is yet to be fully understood.

An adjunct to physical exercise that boosts our brain function is the attention we pay to what we are doing. The intensity that it takes to learn a new skill, whether mental or physical, engages our biology in a positive way. Just as appreciation can help prevent a narrow view of life, the skill of attention benefits the biology of the brain and awareness continues to provide fresh perspectives.

TUNE IN TO RESONANCE

You tend to notice more details when you travel, especially in a location where you do not understand the language. Your awareness heightens simply to get from place to place and to not get lost. Everything around you is new and interesting. Contrast the thrill of discovery with the almost automatic driving you do around the familiar streets of your neighborhood. How often have you headed out to a new place and discovered that instead you took your usual route toward your workplace? Challenge yourself on your next drive in familiar territory to pretend that you've never seen the street before. What

*do you observe? The world changes constantly—don't
miss the show. Explore the same thing the next time you
take a walk in your neighborhood.*

Researchers found that the second most effective
way to augment brain power is through meditation. Isn't
it curious that we are advised to work out, fully engage
our mind with attention, then shift gears and sit as still
as possible, empty the mind, and keep silent? Amishi Jha
at the University of Miami teaches a type of meditation
in which focus is maintained on an object. Classic mindfulness training in Buddhist and yogic traditions often
starts with focus on the flame of a candle, a flower, or the
breath. The instructions include details about the optimal
position for the body—seated with crossed legs, slightly
arched back, and head balanced atop the spine. No slump-
ing or snoozing allowed. The mind is steady and quiet.
The whole of reality is the object of the breath without
intrusion of mind chatter. Relaxed and alert at the same
time, the freedom from worries, agendas, and schemes has
its own benefit. It is possible to achieve this state of mind
in formal meditation and in less formal ways. The rebels
within and among us are grateful that there is no one for-
mula that works for everyone. However, a quiet moment
of connection with the universe, God, source, or principle
of creation can open the gateway to the freedom and richness of inner peace.

Other studies on the effects of meditation by Richard Davidson at the University of Wisconsin showed
increased brain mass in Tibetan monks who meditated regularly. Increased brain mass relates to the
production of more neurons—the process of neurogenesis—initiated by meditation. Many of the monks
tested had logged 50,000 hours of meditation. A theme

in their practices—along with having trained the mind to be relaxed, alert, and stable—was compassion. If they were shown pictures of someone obviously suffering, the left prefrontal cortex lit up with neuronal activity.[4] This is not to say that other areas of the brain were not involved—brain cells fire all over the various parts—but strong activity was observed in the prefrontal cortex, a site known to be active when someone feels compassionate.

There is an experience in meditation during which compassion arises without the meditator thinking about a specific person, situation, or cause of suffering. In the quietest state of alert relaxation with no mental images or thoughts, something happens that is neither expected nor able to be summoned. The experience is beyond description, as if one is in an entirely different dimension. After returning to an ordinary state of consciousness, one might say, "I was immersed in light, compassion surrounded me, and there was a sense of timelessness. I cannot describe how magnificent this was and how it has changed my awareness of life and reality. I appreciate every breath and every vista." Could such an experience promote new brain cells? Studies indicate that this is in fact the case. The ways that profound spiritual incidents affect the body are also anecdotally described by many as enlivening and healing.

The third type of activity that appears to enhance brain function is playing certain types of video and computer games. These games, which also show up on our cell phones, require complex decision making, skill development, and rapt attention. Curiously, a break in playtime with a walk outside also makes a positive difference. The capacity to change focus and direction is essential. How we move from exercise to attentiveness, from deep quiet to sensory stimulation, are all ways of building our mental capacity.

Research on the Benefits of Appreciation

The intriguing work of the Institute of HeartMath has shown that emotions are reflected in the heart's rhythms. When individuals are hooked up to equipment that can record heart rate and display its variability over time, irregular patterns trace fear, anger, and frustration on the paper; the rhythm of the heart is wildly erratic. When individuals learn to shift to a mode of appreciation in a "heartfelt" manner through specific training, their heart rates respond with distinct changes to "a smooth, harmonious, sine wavelike (coherent) pattern."[5]

The practice of appreciation can be applied to everyday activities and perceived changes in quality of life. Studies with volunteers found that those who focused on gratitude each day, especially by writing down what they were grateful for, reported significantly happier lives. They were interested in life around them and others. They had more energy and exercised an hour and a half more each week than those who did not engage in a practice of appreciation. The gratitude group had fewer episodes of illness and slept better.[6] One possible biochemical explanation for these effects is that a heightened state of feeling happy through appreciation causes more dopamine to be produced in the brain that, in turn, activates areas of the brain responsible for conflict resolution and patterns of complex thinking.[7]

With practice comes sophistication in the methodology of appreciation. Happiness can come from doing a good deed itself rather than from any explicit results. Results are a good thing, too, and sometimes they are direct and tangible. In one study, waitresses wrote a simple "thank you" on the bill they placed on the table. The resultant tips were 11 percent higher when compared with bills that did not have the brief message. If additional information was personally written—say, notice of an upcoming special event in the restaurant—their tips rose 17 to 20 percent higher than blank bills with just the charges.[8]

The Interaction of Awareness and Appreciation

When I am happy my body is healthier and my immune system is stronger. My mind is not consumed by "what ifs" or planning for contingencies of disastrous events. My awareness of the environment, the people in my life, and the newness all around me is constantly enhanced and uplifted. In turn, my appreciation increases, too. The dance enhances my creativity and zest for life. This is good.

THE PRACTICE: APPRECIATION AND AWARENESS

Rather than sitting for this practice, I encourage you to put on your favorite walking shoes and head outside. Take a small notebook and pen with you. Use the first ten minutes of your walk to work out the kinks, breathe, find your stride, and get comfortable moving. As you settle into a pace, enjoy the sensations of movement—swing your legs, roll your feet from heel to toe, reach forward with your arms, and deepen your breath. Now look around with heartfelt appreciation for the world you see. Are there flowers, grasses, trees, ponds or rivers, birds or puppies? Take note of three things you have never seen before or are seeing in a new way. Enjoy your expanded awareness. Let your opened awareness flow into appreciation. As your appreciation grows, allow yourself to experience the further growth of awareness.

Take a break on your walk and sit for a few minutes or duck into a coffee shop to jot down the three things you noticed. What was different? How did you feel in the moment? How can you translate this experience of the dance of appreciation and awareness to your work life, your family life, and your creative endeavors?

You may find it useful to keep your own appreciation and awareness journal. You can begin this activity on the blank note pages at the back of this book. When you have a new insight, note how you plan to use it. To look back at your changes is a joy that illuminates how your life has shifted with the practice.

CHAPTER 2

INTUITION AND ACTION

The only real valuable thing is intuition.

— ALBERT EINSTEIN

A carpet of red-hot coals glowed just inches from my bare toes, so close that I could feel the heat on my face and the front of my entire body. I stood at the edge of this expanse with a group of people a lot like me—some curious, some excited, some nervous at the prospect of "walking the coals," which, I might add, I had no intention of doing. We had come to this seminar to learn about fire walking from one of the world's foremost fire-walking gurus. But to actually do it? Not me. The coal bed stretched 15 feet in front of me, but it looked like a football field from my horrified perspective. My friends had invited me to go along with them for this unusual program. Would I go? Sure. Would I walk? No way.

As a cell biologist well acquainted with the reality of searing heat versus skin cells, I had come as an observer only, equipped with equal amounts of natural and professional curiosity and skepticism. In my work, I used an electron microscope to witness the most intimate view of cell life and death. But since my own brush with mortality, I had broadened my focus to include dimensions beyond the familiar scope of life and laboratory. Open to a new and deeper understanding of cell life and healing mechanisms, in the two years since the near-death experience, I'd discovered a diverse world of healing practices, traditions, and rituals; some stranger and more mystical than others. This would include fire walking.

Friends had told me about Tolly Burkan, who was presenting a fire-walking seminar not far from where I lived. Tolly started teaching fire walking in the 1970s and retired in 2008. He and his students have led some three million people over hot coals. Executives in such companies as Microsoft, American Express, and MetLife include fire walking in their development seminars. I was fortunate to be at a fire walk with Tolly himself in the mid-1980s.

Only minutes before actually facing the fire, I listened intently to Tolly Burkan's talk. He told us that he had been "transformed" by the fire-walking experience, and that his goal was to help others learn to conquer the fears that held them back in life. Fire walking, he explained, offered a way to use deep intuition and action to experience an exhilarating release from fear. That seemed incomprehensible to me as I looked out the window of the comfortable lecture room to the tower of burning sticks and branches soon to be embers. I felt safe in my observational mode with absolutely no plans to set foot on any hot coals. I had driven my own car so, if need be, I could make a quick exit.

Tolly described the risks and dangers that we—or the fire walkers, anyway—would encounter. He explained how to listen for our intuitive sense and let it guide our action. If we envisioned ourselves walking the fire and our "gut" was peaceful, at ease, and relaxed, then it was a clear internal message that we would safely cross the fire, he said. If that internal sense constricted, recoiled, or knotted in fear, it would not be safe. In other words, you could trust your gut feeling—but you had to listen clearly for it and let neither fear nor foolhardiness cloud the message. In one state of mind, we resonate with our inner wisdom, and in the other, we experience dissonance with our deep self.

His words rang in my head as we left the lecture hall—left the comfort of merely hearing or thinking about walking on fire to stand outside and watch Tolly's assistants carefully spread the coals with long-handled rakes. We arranged ourselves in a loose circle around the perimeter of the glowing embers. We held hands and anyone who wanted to walk could leave the circle, approach a designated entry point to the stretch of coals, and commence the walk down the 15-foot runway of embers.

There was a pause, and then one woman stepped calmly onto the coals and strode the distance at a brisk but not panicked pace. She stepped off at the end of the path with a look of wonder and joy on her face. Her feet were fine. A couple did the same thing with the same result. Then another woman shifted slightly forward as if to be next. She had a physical disability that required she use forearm crutches to walk. Perhaps sensing her intention, Tolly looked squarely at her and declared that only those who could walk unassisted should attempt the fire walk. He did not explain why. Not heeding his warning, in a flash, she zipped out of the group and moved with surprising speed onto the coals. She made it about a third of the way and started screaming. Several of Tolly's assistants rushed barefoot into the fire and grabbed her. They carried her to an adjacent building to administer first aid, and she was soon taken to the hospital with severe burns. Fireside, everything stopped. No one spoke; we were all frozen in shock and gripped by the very kind of fear we were attempting to conquer. The power of the heat was vivid for us now. The seriousness of this venture couldn't be clearer. Tolly was calm but obviously shaken as he matter-of-factly announced that we had three minutes to head across the fire, after which he would close the event.

Something within me leapt, and it was not my observational, analytical mind. I stepped out of the group, moved to the entry point, and, without hesitation, strode onto the glowing embers. It felt like walking on velvet. I experienced no heat, no burning, just an exhilarating sense of floating and moving—until the last step. I had taken about ten good strides to cross the coals. On the last step I thought, *What am I doing? Why aren't my feet burning?* With that thought, it seemed that my left foot plunged out of whatever state I was in and into the fire of reality. Sudden, searing heat and pain shot through it. By then I was off the fire and sloshing around in a pool of cold water that was provided at the end of the embers. A blister rose on the little toe on my left foot; cold evidence that I had not dreamed walking the fire. I had, indeed, accomplished the journey.

An aftershock of emotions charged through me. I was exhilarated that I had walked on fire, and yet I was aghast that I had moved so quickly, so intuitively. A wave of horror shuddered in my bones as I remembered the woman on crutches who burned her feet so badly. But I also realized that my experience had been quite different. Both my overly analytical mind and my fear had held me back at the fire's edge initially. Like the unfortunate woman before me, I, too, had acted suddenly, from all appearances headed for the same painful fate. Why had I stepped forward onto the coals after what had just happened to her? It wasn't because I felt determined to do it, or hopeful, or even desperate to prove myself. It was because I felt suddenly clear and certain—and this was a physical as well as a mental sensation—that it was safe to go and the time was immediate. I can't explain it, but I knew intuitively that I would be safe. That sensation of deep clarity had carried me across the coals unscathed—well, almost.

The point of Tolly's work had hit home for me: as impossible as it was to explain why my feet didn't burn on the coals, it was possible to learn to listen for intuition and trust it as an expression of an authentic voice of mind, body, and spirit. It isn't required that we walk hot coals to develop this inner guide. Some cultivate this reassuring connection through simple mindful living—learning to listen closely to life—or through meditation, yoga, or other physical and spiritual practices. For others, a sudden life crisis—a serious illness or loss—brings the inner voice forward with intuitive wisdom.

What Is Intuition?

Intuition may seem nothing more than an inexplicable hunch or mysterious sense that nudges us toward certain choices or actions. Indeed, there is some element of mystery to intuition; it can't be completely explained in scientific terms. We can't see intuition on a brain scan, as we can some other neurological functions and states of mind. We haven't identified where intuition lives in the brain—or even that it resides only there. We can't track it on an EKG as we can the electrical impulses of the heart. But there is much more to intuition than what we *don't* know.

When we look closely at the intricate mechanisms for communication and interaction between the brain, mind, body, and spirit, we see that intuition is part of an elaborate internal "intelligence operation" in which cells collect, process, and disseminate information constantly. Just as our sense of sight allows us to take in our surroundings, our intuitive sense continually monitors our internal and external environments, processes the information, and makes it available to us in subtle ways. Intuition may alert us to a shift in circumstances or emotional energy in someone we know, or nudge us in a direction with everyday choices we make. We may follow our intuitive hunches and make highly effective choices in our work. Or we may sense an undiagnosed physical illness. The more attuned we are to our intuitive sense, the more consciously we can receive its messages and act from this deeper awareness.

Skeptics point out that the reliability of hunches and nudges run a gamut from total error to eerily correct, and it is true that sometimes what we think is intuition can lead to costly mistakes.[1] Others insist that intuition is highly reliable and can be accessed through training. Wisely, the most recent trend has been to acknowledge intuition, and to refine our use of this "subtle sense" in decisions that affect our health and happiness.[2] Whether or not we can explain intuition scientifically, it is no less real than muscle and bone—or thought, for that matter.

Our ancestors relied upon the gifts of intuition for their survival. Among indigenous peoples of today, practices that cultivate access to subtle messages from the environment or from each other are valued and encouraged. Certain members of the community are often remarkably gifted in those abilities. Historically, in Australia members of an aboriginal tribe used smoke signals to alert another group, many miles away, that someone would be sending a message solely through thoughts—what we would call mental telepathy. The natural intuitive in the far group would be summoned to "listen" for the message. Contrary to the impression given by old Western movies, for this tribe at least, smoke signals were not patterns to be read like Morse code but rather signals that a message was to be received. Smoke was the ringer on the phone alerting the receiver to a message on its way through intuitive channels.[3]

In contemporary life, from the kitchen to the boardroom to the emergency room, we see people whose success reflects more than training alone; intuitive skills distinguish their work or interactions with others. At a glance, their remarkable success might seem to be a combination of old-fashioned smarts and good luck. A closer look at the intuitive process shows something very different. We cultivate our intuitive sense in many ways through everyday experience.

From Hard Science to Healing Action

The field of science, for all its necessary focus on process and proof, is surprisingly dependent on the intuitive strengths of researchers and theorists. One of the nation's leading cancer researchers today is celebrated for his intuitive sense, which has led to significant advances in cancer therapies. Colleagues say Carlo Croce has remarkable scientific instincts. "If you spread out five things in front of him, he can almost unerringly pick the one which is going to work," says Webster Cavenee, director of the Ludwig Institute for Cancer Research in San Diego. "He can smell something interesting, and he's almost never wrong."[4] I didn't realize it at the time, but my earlier days of working as a scientist involved honing my intuitive skills. As part of my characteristic way of beginning a project, I would look at several different research approaches that we might consider. After a rather brief review, I would feel an intuitive sense regarding which approach would lead to reliable data and useful answers. That seemingly non-analytical ability coupled with my formal knowledge and training as a scientist allowed me to complete and publish my research at a markedly faster pace than is typical because there weren't as many false starts or dead ends. However, coupled with that intuitive sense—or an integral part of it—was extensive prior work searching the scientific literature, highly analytical data processing, and mathematical computation. In other words, I'd been immersed for years in the growing body of information in a field I was passionate about, and I was able to draw from both my conscious and unconscious store of information to inform my intuitive sense about research subjects and the approaches most likely to be effective. My track record of success gave me the confidence to follow intuitive cues, though I wouldn't have described it that way at the time. Looking back, I realize that I did not consciously set out to use intuition; in fact, I took it for granted. But it was so strongly there, and now I can identify and appreciate its role. I encourage you to reflect on how intuition has already served you and how you have drawn on it by taking a minute to use the following practice.

TUNE IN TO RESONANCE

Reflect on a particularly successful action in your life. How much did you rely on your analytical skills? How much did your intuition contribute? Allow yourself to realize and appreciate how you combined intuition and analysis to make your actions successful. Perhaps there is a situation you face today that requires action. How can you combine both approaches to move forward in the best possible way?

As my healing gift expanded into a full-time career, I was keenly aware of the need to pay careful attention to intuition before acting. Other healers, including those who practice conventional Western medicine, speak similarly of how they develop intuitive gifts. These may appear as "knowings" that carry the intensity of certainty about how to proceed with a client. An out-of-the-ordinary visual experience or a subtle yet pertinent message may be the vehicle of intuitive knowing for the healer.

When I am working, typically I feel pain in my own body at the site of a client's malaise. During a recent hospital call, the client had undergone the removal of a kidney in preparation for a kidney transplant. Although she had been released from the hospital and seemed to recuperate reasonably well, she still had severe pain in her midsection that sent her back to the hospital. Pancreatitis—a pancreatic inflammation—was the problem. By the time I was called to do some energy healing, the pancreatitis had subsided. However, even a slight elevation of her head caused severe retching and vomiting. She was utterly miserable. As I worked, I began to feel nauseated. I could tell that this was not an emotional reaction to her situation, but a connection with her physical state.

I only allow myself to feel the malady of others to the point that I can understand what they are experiencing, albeit in a milder form. This is a type of empathic listening that includes a kinesthetic sense in my own body. Once I feel attuned to the mental and physical state of my client, I consciously stop allowing their illness to so profoundly affect me. I also consciously remove whatever I have picked up from them by using a visualization of spirals of light circulating around me. Then, and only then, do I proceed with the healing session.

From numerous conversations with healers, friends, and clients, it seems that most of us intuitively and unknowingly pick up other people's angst and even their physical symptoms all the time.[5] To be aware of this receptivity in ourselves and to know that we can release or clear that entanglement will allow us to be effectively compassionate in a healing sense and free of others' issues at the same time. In the case of my nauseous client, once I was attuned to her condition, as soon as I felt the symptom, I consciously stopped bringing it into my body and cleared my energy so that I could continue to assist her. We all need to fine-tune the way our intuitive sense processes incoming information and delivers it to us!

How Ordinary Knowing
Becomes Extraordinary Knowing

Although I was awakened to my deeper powers of intuition, first through an almost fatal accident and then later through my experience walking the coals, I assure you that you can tap into this channel of inner wisdom through a calmer, quieter practice of your own design.

I often receive letters and e-mails from former students and clients, and I am always delighted—though not at all surprised—to hear their personal stories of deepening intuitive experiences and the beneficial actions that have resulted when they trust that inner guide. They describe many different paths to this awakening, but the origins of intuition are common to us all.

Where does our "way of knowing" come from? Let's take a brief look at the ordinary ways in which we all receive information through a combination of mind, body, and spiritual sources.

Our minds are constantly sorting out input from our basic senses of sight, sound, touch, taste, and smell. Some of our earliest lessons develop associations with positive experiences and their accompanying stimuli. Favorite foods, the smell of the ocean, or the sound of crickets on a summer night—so many sensory cues carry a connotation of "familiar and favorable" for us even at the most subtle levels. We also discover how to avoid pain through other sensory warnings. If you've ever touched a thistle plant and felt the sting of its sharp, barbed leaf, you can be sure that you stored that lesson away for future reference.

Physiological activity, which includes the internal activity of our cells, hormones, and other biochemicals, is another major source of information, which we'll examine shortly. In addition to these conventional information sources, intuition draws from other sources that we cannot see or truly explain: dreams, memory, extrasensory or psychic energy from other people, and spiritual or universal sources. Although scientific interest and research into this unexplained link is growing, for now it remains a gap in any scientific understanding of intuition. As we've discussed before, we can acknowledge the gap and continue nonetheless to study what we know lies on both sides.

Altered states of awareness in varying degrees can be part of the approach to intuition. This is particularly true among indigenous healers. In my direct experience with healers in Bali, I learned that they can enter an altered state solely through meditation and see into cellular structures even when they have never heard about cells or seen cell images in books or through microscopes. In other cultures, hallucinogens are sometimes used in special ways to reach those altered states in brain functioning. Although substances such as peyote or ayahuasca have opened altered mind states for many, the use of hallucinogens has not been part of my path. Meditation or healing ceremonies have been my conduit to profound states of altered awareness, and I recommend them.

What is it about the nonanalytical parts of our brains that come forward when we enter a state of lucid dreaming or light trance? How is it that the resulting information can prove to be spot-on reliable? Perhaps we open to information that is ordinarily outside the limitations of conventional understanding. Seers and shamans in these other cultures are counted on as reliable sources for the community and for individuals. Although they may not be 100 percent correct, they are dependable enough to maintain a revered position. These healers, who train in their own traditions to be of benefit to their communities, have learned to attune their intuitive senses to the deep resonance of the cells and systems of the body. If something is amiss, they sense what is wrong and what is needed to bring healing.

Sometimes the shaman works through the patient's own knowing. I learned from one patient about an indigenous healer who performed a ceremony for her mother who was quite desperately ill and suffering from tremors and constant shaking. During the ceremony, the sick woman dropped into a profound trance state and, in her mind, a bear showed her a forested place where there were special herbs that could help her. As she partially woke from the trance, she ran into the nearby forest and was drawn farther and farther to a place where the low-growing vegetation was trampled down. She picked the flattened herbs and made teas of them. The infusion cured her completely. She had become an intuitive channel for the information she needed to find the herbs and make the curative tea.

These subtle senses can become guides to action as we develop awareness of them and learn to determine their trustworthiness. We may start with that gut sense we explored with regard to the fire-walking experience, and continue to develop additional skill with increasingly subtle intuitive messages. We learn what intuition feels like for ourselves and how to interpret our own unique nudges.

Although not always expressed so dramatically as in fire walking and bear visions, we all have intuition and sources of intuitive knowledge that grow and deepen throughout life. Let's first learn how the body generates the information flow within itself, and then train ourselves in more profound ways of developing our connection with the inner voice and wisdom of intuitive guidance.

Under ordinary circumstances, I have found that certain qualities of mind accompany the resonance of authentic intuition and help me distinguish this deeper guidance from its cousin, impulsivity. These qualities

include: neutrality, certain physical and spiritual aware-
nesses, and a careful reality check. Take the time (and it
doesn't take much) to pause before an answer or action
is required of you. Listen for these qualities; they can
help you discern between true intuition and impulsivity or egoic tendency.

Neutrality: Intuition is impartial. A neutral state of
mind allows intuition to emerge freely, and intuition
itself imparts a sense of neutrality. When we are pushing for a particular outcome, attached to a result, or
grasping at a specific option as the only way, we are
unable to hear the deeper inner voice of intuition over
the cacophony of other input. It is a good practice to
find a neutral "place" in your thinking. Neutral does not
imply that you do not care, but that you trust a higher
order to guide you to the most efficacious outcome. And
by "place" I don't mean you have to physically remove
yourself to a soundproof room (you'll just bring your
internal cacophony with you). We can create our neutral place of listening in the moment, anywhere, simply
by choosing to set aside the noisy voices of intense
attachment to outcome for a few moments of quiet
reflection and neutrality. Don't panic; you do not have
to abandon your desire, but simply ask it to wait quietly
while you check to see if the coast is clear. Your intuition, after all, is essentially on your side; if you are to
act effectively in the complexity of circumstances, your
actions will be precise, limited, and valuable. Intuitive
actions are that.

Tune In to Resonance

*There are many cues you can use to help yourself let
go of a specific outcome for this moment. A statement*

such as "I seek the most benevolent outcome," or visualizing yourself free-falling gently into a soft, safe place, may be helpful.

Physicality: More often than not, I feel the nudge of intuition in a physical sense—at the edge of a tactile sensation, as if I am drawn toward something, yet not pushed or pulled. The feeling comes in varying degrees. Others have described the sensation of strong intuition in similar near-physical terms. A client described a challenging change in her life as a series of intuitive moments that felt "as if the seas were parting, and I was drawn along a clear path." Sometimes an image will come to you as a clear visual sensation of direction. Although the intuition may be totally correct, it is not necessarily an easy action or smooth sailing as you proceed. "Easy" is not a sensory experience that necessarily connotes correct intuition. When someone describes a calling in life, the calling is rarely remarkable for its ease, but the same intuitive source behind it holds the answer to whatever challenges may arise; a calling is intuition in action. You may find the winds blowing you where you most need to go, but the seas can be rough in the midst of it.

TUNE IN TO RESONANCE

Allow your mind to freely imagine the path that lies ahead—what comes to mind first? Whatever the nature of it—a parting sea, a winding mountain path, or a deep forest—let go of the need to react, and simply observe it with curiosity and openness to learning more.

Spirituality: One of the most reliable ways to enhance your intuitive knowing is to continue your spiritual practice and to expand it, going deeper in your meditation. The next chapter will look at how our chosen spiritual connection informs the journey of healing. I find that the deeper my meditation, the more effective the healing work. Meditation also affects the way I live in the everyday world with increasing calmness, understanding, and zest for life. I experienced these changes before I knew anything about the teachings of a particular spiritual tradition. Once I began to seriously study comparative texts of religious traditions, I found context for many of my experiences. The lived experience came first and the understanding much later. This may be the case for you as well, or you may find that study leads to experience. How humbling to honor the many paths that lead to authentic spiritual connection—and to honor yours.

In embracing spirituality as a source for intuitive guidance here are three key aspects:

1. How we see ourselves and how we imagine the universe. *Who am I in this moment? How do I experience my connection with the nature and the flow of all things? Am I acting in accord with my deepest spiritual intuition?*

2. How we engage in meditation (the touchstone of intuition). *Is my meditation vital to my everyday life? Does my meditation grow and change as I develop spiritually? Am I willing to allow my meditation to shift from duty to delight? How are my meditative experiences informing my intuition?*

3. How we act in relationships and community. *Is my life in the workplace and with my family*

congruent with my spirituality? Do I cherish the
flow of intuitive wisdom in the simplest of daily
activities? Have I learned to listen to intuition with
ease and grace in all aspects of my life?

Reality Check: Not every nudge is an accurate intuitive message. While the qualities of neutrality, physicality, and spiritual listening are crucial in developing reliable intuition, it is also appropriate to check out those intuitive calls to action with another person. Talk out loud about what you have experienced and what you plan to do about it. Of course, it is important to choose your confidant carefully. A spiritual leader, therapist, well-grounded friend, or wise family member may be the one. Ultimately, it comes back to one's own deepest discernment as the consequences, good or not so good, of every choice rest on each of us individually.

Another aspect of reality checks includes those uncomfortable situations when someone tells you what you should do based on *their* intuition. That message might resonate perfectly with you or it might not. Take time to sense if the information is indeed in your best interest. One very good measure of validity in such a situation is the presence of compassion accompanying the intuition and the ability of the action to serve the highest good.

TUNE IN TO RESONANCE

Take a deep breath and let go fully. Relax and let the quality of compassion arise within you. Allow yourself to rest in that place, and notice how it moves within you. Invite a deeper sense of connection with the source of compassion, that universal quality, to touch you and expand the resonance with your intuition and the best action possible in any situation.

Intuition That Leads to Unanticipated Outcomes

My experiences with healers and shamans in other countries have been a continual series of lessons in how intuition and action are closely intertwined and essential to each other. I am not skilled in the acquisition of new languages, so I've had to make sense of many situations without the benefit of having comprehended a conversation. Intuition has been an essential guide in these situations.

Working with shamans in other countries has never been a five-star hotel experience for me. This is not a complaint; I've thoroughly relished my off-the-beaten-track experiences. I plunged into these opportunities without any particular preparation. I was given no syllabus, no idea whatsoever of what I would be doing or what would be required of me. I accepted the invitations purely on the basis of my own intuitive sense and each part of these experiences was an exercise in following intuition.

The first trip to Bali included a surprising connection with a shaman who lived far from any Western resorts or lodging. Through Budi, my translator and trusted guide, she invited me to stay in her family compound, which I did on my second trip to the island. Budi dropped me off at her place, a series of small cottages with a central area where everyone ate together and congregated. This place was on a remote road in the midst of acres of beautifully terraced rice fields and steamy jungle gorges. I slept in a tiny room on a wooden plank with a long body bolster to drape my body over and only a sarong as a cover. The bathroom was in a separate cottage and used by all ten of us who lived in the family compound. This bathroom had an open tank of water that I could dip a pan into and pour water over myself to bathe. The toilet was a hole at ground level and there were wiggly wormy things squirming around the wet floor. I sometimes wondered what I was doing there, just as I had wondered what I was doing when I found myself standing at the edge of red-hot coals.

One morning when dawn was barely breaking and everyone was asleep, including the roosters, I heard my name called in a shrill voice: "Jo . . . iiiii . . . ce!" The call woke me from an exhausted sleep, and I bolted up to open my door a crack and peek out. There was Jero Tapakan, my shaman, my teacher, at the step calling me to go. I considered feigning sleep and a deaf ear, but I felt the nudge within to join her. Quickly, I threw on my clothes—that is, a T-shirt and sarong. I slapped my flip-flops on my feet and figured that we were having tea or going to meditate in this early hour. Not so, however, as Jero took off toward the back of the compound, peering back to make sure I was following. We left the cottages behind and headed down a rice field, a part of the place I had not noticed before.

Soon the rice field was no longer level, but dropped steeply down and down. At one point we turned abruptly to our left and a few feet ahead was a human-sized statue in the middle of a carved rock shrine. The statue was one I had never seen in all my trekking around Bali, but I now know that it depicted Sangyang Widi Wasa, one of the Balinese images of the Supreme Being. We stopped there as Jero (the title of my host, and the more general title of a healer in Bali) performed a short ceremony. We then proceeded along a verdant ledge, overgrown with vines and bushes but no rice plants. Below us was a steep drop-off to a river and jungle. We were eye to eye with the tops of palm trees on one side of the steep path. Suddenly, my feet went out from under me, and I was tumbling, rolling toward the edge of the precipice. I was in trouble before I even realized it. Jero was a tiny woman, about 70 years old at that time, but she grabbed me, stopped my rolling, and hung on to me with a strength and tenacity that I will never forget. I owe my unbroken limbs and very probably my life to her.

After we caught our breath, we finished the climb to a rock face with a cave entrance and a waterfall gushing out of the rock. Jero motioned for me to undress and bathe in the water. It was refreshingly cold, with some other-worldly quality. I was euphoric. I felt as if I could have flapped my arms and flown from the place. This was more than just a quick shower under a pounding stream of clear water. I was lifted. I was transformed. I was in a state of bliss. Then I settled out of the bliss into an ordinary state, as I got dressed and waited as Jero also bathed in the water-fall. The world, however, never quite looked the same. The surroundings became luminous, the dangerous ledge was no longer a threat; it was merely a ledge. My feet felt sure and firm on the path.

We turned to walk back, but to my surprise, did not go up the rice field in the same way as we had descended. Along the new route, we found a banana tree with ripe fruit. Jero whipped a knife out of somewhere in the folds of her sarong and whacked off a bunch of gloriously golden bananas. I will never forget the happy grin that spread across her face as she shouldered the bunch and we con-tinued our circuitous route back to the family compound. Two days later when Budi arrived to bail me out of any trouble I might have created, he listened intently to Jero describe what we had done and relayed that the name of the place we had gone was The Angel's Place. It was called that "because angels are often seen there." I had certainly felt them, felt their spirit, and was renewed, blessed, and happy that I had responded to my intuition in moments when practical considerations might have had me do otherwise. The translator also said that Jero had performed a sacred initiation for me, and that the gods had accepted me. I will never know what might have been the outcome if they had refused me.

In retrospect, I can recall those moments of intuitive nudges—I can still feel the near-physical tug of them. There was the choice to stay in the family compound when hotel comforts beckoned at a resort just 50 miles away. The moment Jero's eerie call to me pulled me from a sound sleep, out into an unexpected adventure—and even more unexpected outcome. I'm reminded of the fire walk and the way—just as in Bali—circumstances had presented me with someone who had provided the opportunity and invitation, but I had a choice—and intuition had moved me to respond. As I have said, I have no explanation for the fact that my feet didn't burn (except for that little toe). And I marvel still at the fact that I survived the fall on that steep mountain ledge in Bali, saved only by Jero's reach in that split second. At these times, and no less in everyday situations, intuitive guidance can lead us to unexpected and rewarding outcomes.

THE PRACTICE: INTUITION AND ACTION

When there are questions about your life choices, direction, or health, enter a quiet state of mind by using an image of what is, for you, a peaceful place. In nature perhaps, visualize yourself stepping into a verdant glade where old oak trees create a canopy of spreading branches. Walk past tree by tree as you unwind from tension, then at the base of one of the trees discover a comfortable bench with cushions on which you can recline. Rest there and allow the sacred glen to hold you in a neutral and receptive mode. In the quiet calm of your mind, an intuitive nudge may arise. If you prefer, pose a neutral question inviting insight or guidance: for example, "What is the best training to take that will further my work of service?"

Once an intuitive nudge arises here is how I test it to decide if I will act. I imagine in detail what a plan of action would entail. If it involves travel, for example, I see myself packing the suitcase, catching the shuttle, arriving at the airport, and so on. The key here is what my body does with this sequence of images. Am I energized or not? Do I feel alive and eager, or has my body become heavy with a lifeless feeling? That semi-numb sense is a sure sign that I'm off-track. But the energized and vital body sense is a reliable indicator that action is appropriate.

In your special quiet place, begin to visualize in detail the action you are considering.

Are you tense or relaxed? Anxious or eager? Are you breathing deeply or has your breathing become shallow? If you feel relaxed and eager and your breath is even and smooth, then it is a good sign for reliable intuition to develop.

One final reality check: is the action possible and sensible? You always have a choice and must use your good sense in making that choice. If common sense says "no" then accept that continued practice will deliver the insight needed for eventual action.

Practice with simple intuition/action situations. When an ordinary question comes up, pause, take a deep breath, and remember the quality of intuition that is a basic part of yourself. With another breath relax in the moment and listen for the intuitive guidance that arises within you. You can invite your intuitive senses to expand and work for you. Enjoy how they quietly guide your next business meeting, your next travel adventure, or your response to family matters. Regardless of your circumstances, when you allow actions to be guided by intuition you will engage the fullness of your capacity as a conscious being.

CHAPTER 3

PRESENCE AND COMMUNICATION

At the very frontier of science new ideas are emerging
that challenge . . . how we define ourselves. . . .
human beings are far more extraordinary
than an assemblage of flesh and bones.

— LYNNE MCTAGGART

Healing is a natural quality of the universe. Renewal and regeneration occur again and again in biological beings as well as in star systems. From the turmoil of the collisions of galaxies and the annihilation within black holes, elements are recycled into newly birthed stars. This universal pattern plays out in our bodies—puny and infinitesimally small on a galactic scale, but gigantic compared to the electrons, atoms, and molecules that cluster to create our living, breathing form.

The primordial grit of creation also engendered a self-replicating world of biological diversity complete with innate healing properties. Those natural aspects reflect a creative presence everywhere. The more we practice presence—both with the body and with the eternal essence of creation—and develop a reliable means of connection and communication, the more our inborn gifts of healing can flourish. Undeniably, healing is within us as a natural biological function. When our bodies suffer from injury or disease, we seek to enhance those inner resources. The process of becoming a facilitator of healing involves learning the communication style—the language—of Spirit and the language of the body. To develop this skill, we start with the body.

The language of the cells resides at an interface deep within each cell: a nanoworld where energy and matter meet, where vibration and molecules interact, where the original "star stuff" flying through the far reaches of the universe came together to create atoms that bonded and molecules that clustered and responded to the pulse of life. From a unique series of events the human species emerged, notable for its diversity, yet built upon a common structure.

Underlying our personal individuality and uniqueness is that universal basic structure that is uncanny in its similarity with other life forms. In fact, we share half of our genetic code with bananas. Now that is humbling. One of our closest mammalian relatives is the chimpanzee, whose DNA sequences are 98 percent identical to ours. The question arises: what makes us human? To date, no one has fully solved this mystery. It is a useful inquiry to ask oneself, *How do I understand my humanity?*

You started life as a single cell, the offering of genetic material from both your mother and your father. During nine months of gestation, your cells divided rapidly and began to cluster in specific locations with more and more specific jobs. Eventually you were a fully functioning baby body with all the necessary organs and systems ready for the outside world. After birth, cells continued to divide and you grew into a standard-issue adult human body of between 75 and 100 trillion cells. This is a well-organized system, neither random nor scattered, but highly structured and efficient. Different types of cells have varied life cycles along with their special jobs. Sustainability rules, however. Cells are the original environmentalists, repairing, reusing, and recycling matter and energy in their molecular milieu. Given all this complexity and all these massive numbers of cells, how do they communicate with each other?

Each cell busily at work in its respective tissue receives information from the entire body: the biochemistry of communication is refined, accurate, and universal throughout the body, as a growing body of research literature has established. Hormones, glycoproteins, and neuropeptides carry information through the bloodstream to all cells. Cell signaling is one of the hottest topics of current research in cell biology. In these new studies, scientists have begun to identify the materials and means by which molecules are pulled from the cell's environment through the cell membrane and into specific areas of the cell. Some interact at other locations within each cell. Errors in cell signaling are known to be involved in serious and sometimes life-threatening illnesses such as heart disease, cancer, and arthritis.[1] In addition, cells also communicate with each other through direct cell-to-cell contact. Adjacent cells send out small tubes, called nano-tubes,[2] that exchange information directly, cell by cell. Our cells maintain resonance with each other and the whole body through these extraordinary means.

Another equally precise information modality in the body is the recently discovered action of dying cells that pinch off a tiny vesicle from their cell membrane. That vesicle touches nearby cells and communicates that cell death has happened. That message in mice with athero-sclerosis causes repair of the lesions left by the dead cell in the damaged blood vessel. Similar studies with cells of human umbilical veins show that a complex cascade of biochemical events results from messages carried by vesi-cles of the dying cells. At the end of the chain, a molecule is formed and recruits cells whose specific function is to repair the site.[3]

These examples illustrate that one of our most basic natural attributes is communication, which in turn establishes our presence as a being, an individual. Expanding from that basis, we make contact with each other using skills of communication that include modali-ties similar to those of our internal cellular communities. We sometimes communicate with direct touch, not with nanotubes as cells do, but with our hands and other body parts. Several forms of physical energy activate our sen-sory systems: vibration creates sound, which our ears translate into communication; light transmits images, which we experience as vision. All this information is passed as biochemical packets between brain cells as it shapes our perception of the world.

TUNE IN TO RESONANCE

Take a moment to notice your hands. How do they look? Touch the tips of your fingers on the left hand with the right hand and pause to feel the subtlety of changes in pressure, texture, and warmth that transfers from one hand to the other. How do you communicate with your touch? What messages have you received from others via their touch? Have you appreciated the variety of communications that proceed from simple touch?

In certain situations, we rely on intermediaries to bridge a communication gap. In any large business, the person who answers the phone may have the connection we need, but frequently does not. Sometimes, that exasperated "Let me talk to your supervisor" can get us in direct contact with someone who can make the required changes. I recently transferred my business phone service from an office of nine years to a new location. Although I was assured that the messaging service would work flawlessly during my one-month vacation between closing the old office and opening the new one, the message for incoming calls was: "Sorry, this number has been changed." It took an entire day of fussing around with one person after another who did not know how to fix the problem, until I finally worked my way up the chain to a supervisor who could do what was necessary. She had my voice mail operating correctly in minutes.

Access to the connection we need is also important in the spiritual sphere. Frustration ensues when we do not believe that we have direct access to the energy or consciousness of the universal source. A few years after my near-death experience, and early in my work as a healer, I had taken a class on the use of crystals for healing. I became entranced by the beauty of crystals, the lore about them, and the variety of their beautiful colors and shapes. I read books about how to use crystals for spiritual work. I spent money acquiring a collection of large and small specimens of quartz, tourmaline, celestine, citrine, amethyst, garnet, galena, lapis, labradorite, opal, peridot, and on and on. I had a particularly beautiful (and expensive) aquamarine pendant that I loved and always wore. I was so attached to the pendant as a source of connection to healing that I could not leave it behind when I traveled to the Philippines to work with a native healer.

The year was 1986, two years after I had left the laboratory and begun working full time as a healer. I stayed in Baguio, a small mountain town about six hours by slow bus from Manila. For two months my daily routine was early-morning mass with my hosts, followed by two hours of meditation; then breakfast, followed by assisting the healer for the rest of the day until dark. Thirty people might show up to see him for a few minutes, he was so revered and so effective with his healing gift. Those early morning meditations at the parish were some of the most significant I had experienced up to that time. Divine presence was tangible, joyful, and emotionally touching; drawing butterflies and dragonflies to fly to me light on my hands. I had no fear and no grasping, and bliss abounded.

The healer I worked with was a profoundly devoted Catholic and had mentored me for several months as I worked with him in his home office in Baguio. My life was immersed in a Philippine healing flow. Visitors from Europe or the United States looked strange to me. One day, unexpectedly, he announced that I was to spend just under a week in a Carmelite convent outside of Baguio for a personal retreat. The convent was situated at the end of a remote road with a view of wild mountainous terrain and a glimpse of ocean on a clear day. I was welcomed to the guest quarters by Sister Bernadette, the one nun appointed to interface with the world outside the convent and with anyone from the outside who came as a guest. I was the only visitor at the time.

My five-day stay in the guest quarters was an exercise in stark simplicity. The bed was a slab of wood with barely a cover and no padding. The room was bare except for pictures of Jesus and Mary. Fortunately, the bathroom had a flush toilet. For a shower, there was an angled pipe high on the wall through which cold water drizzled when the faucet was turned on. Meals were very simple: Two times each day I would go downstairs to a large room where Sister Bernadette brought me rice and some fruit to eat. She would sit and converse with me for a short while. I found her a wise and compassionate presence, the brightest part of the day. After she heard my story of near-death, how I left my profession to jump into the mystery of trying to help people heal, she gave me her notated and underlined copy of the writings of Saint John of the Cross. I still have that book and have treasured it these many decades later.

Days went by and I continued to mellow and adapt to the quiet, contemplative flow of the life in the convent. Each afternoon I could hear the chatter and laughter of the nuns as they had their one hour to break silence. What a pleasant uproar! Each morning at dawn we were summoned by a bell to the chapel and a local priest lead the mass. The sisters sang in the sweetest tones and peered at me from behind a lattice barrier, their gaze quickly averted if I looked back. One morning I was in the guest quarters bathroom facing the drizzling cold water for my morning wash before 6 A.M. mass. I had removed the silver chain with the aquamarine crystal from my neck and hung it carefully on a nail inside the entrance to the bathroom. My clothes were draped on another protruding nail. As I was about to endure the cold water stream, a thought filled my otherwise quiet mind. I did not hear a voice, but the thought was almost as tangible as an actual voice. *Stop using crystals. You have learned everything you can from them. You no longer need them. Pure presence is sufficient.*

I dismissed the idea, and figured that I had been eating too much rice and too many mangoes, or had simply spent too much time alone. At that very moment, the aquamarine crystal abruptly and spontaneously shattered into pieces. As I picked up the fragments, I said, "Okay, okay, I'm listening." The communication was clear, multisensory, and impressive. I had loved crystals and had learned how to focus energy and how to hold a precise energy vibration by using them, but they were training wheels, not the source of healing. Clearly I had sufficiently learned the necessary lessons. Graduation arrived as a moment of crystalline intensity.

TUNE IN TO RESONANCE

What kind of communication with presence have you already experienced? Perhaps this would be an appropriate time to start a notebook and jot down a few words or outline of how you have been in touch with presence. What has opened you to communication within yourself and with the universe?

The communication with presence is not always so dramatic. Not that drama is bad, but it is so emphatically humbling. I've learned to listen and trust more and more subtle communication. The awe that comes with such events is part of a numinous incident well-named and described by Rudolf Otto in the early 20th century. He defined the word *numinous* as "the sense of presence much greater than oneself, something Wholly Other, which creates awe."[4]

These unexpected numinous experiences, ones we cannot create out of our own desires, lead us to contemplation. What is this presence? What is the experience of presence? How can we be present and approach presence? How does communication with presence relate to healing?

How Can We Identify Presence?

No one and no group has a complete answer for this question. Most of us have some idea from our religious backgrounds, our personal search, or our direct and authentic experiences. We refer to presence by many names: God, Source, Universe, Emptiness, Luminosity. One direct encounter, however, usually nullifies the need for a precise and final name. The more direct our contact, the smaller our vocabulary becomes until we virtually cannot express what presence is. Words can't get there. Concepts are woefully inadequate, yet our experience stands as a witness to that inexpressible reality. At the same time, we recognize that our own efforts to "be present" are a part of presence. Practicing presence begins as a two-way street, leading ultimately to the experience of no street at all—that is, to the state of oneness, without time, space, or barriers of any kind.

What Is an Experience of Presence Like?

The encounters that people report are even more varied than the descriptive names for presence. Some people have intense visual effects such as seeing colors or shapes. The colors are clear and vibrant, and they often move or swirl. Along with the hue, shapes or images may accompany these inner visions. Fragrant smells and lovely sounds such as harmonious tones or singing happen for some. Body sensations include a light feeling or just the opposite: a very heavy and deeply relaxed feeling in the arms or legs or the entire body. Temperature changes occur, too. Sudden waves of heat may run through the body or a chill may tremble through your core.

Emotional responses are common. Tears of awe flow without warning. Once while I was in Bali, I had the sweet opportunity to meditate with a master jeweler who was also a priest. We had our eyes closed as we sat in a circle and chanted traditional Hindu chants. The sound of pure devotion in the voices of we six was palpable. Tears started silently streaming down my face. The jeweler stopped the chanting and leaned toward me saying, "You are very close to God. How can that be? You are a tourist!" We became friends that very moment.

Additional emotional releases may come as a wave of deep relaxation, as if you never felt so relaxed before in your life. There may be a sense of release of old anxieties, old resentments, and old anger. As the letting go proceeds, a profound love may sweep your senses. This may be directed toward yourself, someone else, or a situation, or it may be completely free flowing.

Letting go of old issues is not one of the easiest processes. I find that in this process it is important to not get carried away with identifying cause and effect, but understand that the communication with presence that releases held traumas is beneficial.

How Can We Approach Presence?

This is an issue of apparent opposites. On the one hand, humility is required; on the other, a certain boldness and positive anticipation is required. The experience of being "on the other side" during my near-death experience was highly instructive. Without any intellectual machinations, I was humbled by such intense feelings of peace and joy while being fully at ease with myself. I'd never been as totally and simply contented as at that moment. The pure and total love of that presence made me feel as if I teetered on the threshold of a vast universe and yet that I was known in that universe. My life had both a precious nature and a limited nature. That life was truly a gift was crystal clear.

I spent years devising meditations that would take my awareness to the "other side"—back into the images and perceptions I had seen. I so longed to return there and have both fullness of presence and communication be the same. I would imagine walking over a rainbow bridge from here to "there." Sometimes it seemed that I could enter that place of bliss, but it was never with the fullness of image or emotion as before. I don't remember how the idea came to me that I could enjoy the presence and union of oneness here and now. In that moment I envisioned reaching up to grab hold of my higher consciousness (for lack of a better description) and pull her into my physical body. A strange sensation came over me. I felt in complete communication with all that is. I felt satisfied, at home, and at peace. Years and years later I learned of the Mahayana Buddhist view that *samsara*, earthly existence, and *nirvana*, paradise or heaven, are one. That translates to the here of ordinary life, relative reality, and the vastness of everything, ultimate reality, being in union. The concept only barely captures the actual experience. It is astounding that such incidents can ever happen to us, and it is closer than we think. Indeed, it is not about thought. It is beyond thought. We cannot grasp or command presence to come to us. Openness is useful, but grace may bless us at any moment.

One of those times of grace happened for me many years ago as I was beginning my work as a healing facilitator and spending parts of the evening in meditation. I had a nubby beige couch under a window in an upstairs room of my home. After tucking my young daughter into bed, I would curl up on this couch, wrapped in a blanket. As a regular practice, I gazed out at the stars and let my breath be slow, deliberate, and conscious. Such simple actions brought a quiet to my being. On this night, as I snuggled into the couch and visualized breathing in the light of the stars, I decided to explore my shadow side. I imagined that I could leap into a darkness that was neither frightening nor horrid, but dark and unknown. I felt physical sensations of walking into cold darkness. The closest experience I remember to the vision was walking into a lava tube at the Ape Caves in southwest Washington. The visionary darkness was a tunnel on level ground with rounded walls, no side passages, no end in sight and no way to see the opening once inside the cave. Unlike the Ape Caves, which ended in a wall, rippled with the solidified flow of lava that had cooled thousands of years ago, the dark tunnel in my vision was different: it had no end. I kept going and going in my search for a way through this darkness, or a passage out, or maybe a shaft of gloriously blessed light.

Here the darkness never ended, and I became increasingly distressed. Frightened and lost, I had no sense of where to go to get out. I could not tell which way was deeper in and which way was out. I stopped with my fear and shuddered at my cavalier decision to "explore the shadow." What had I done to myself? After some time of muttering about my lost state, I finally sat down and thought, *Now what do I do?*

An answer came as quickly as the question. *Make an altar where you are.* In detail I imagined a simple altar and projected it from my mind almost as a hologram in the midst of this dark place. I don't know why I picked the items for the altar but they came quickly. There was a small white table, a simple white cloth, a Christian cross, and a brass bowl containing rose-scented water. As I sat there, I opened my heart to the divine presence, and a radiant light surrounded me. My sense of self lifted and expanded. I sat up straight, took a deep breath, and felt comfort. I felt safe. I felt located, not lost. I felt at peace.

A voice bigger than my own, but not unlike my own seemed to say, *Everywhere is sacred. The universe is full of the presence of Spirit. No matter where you flee, how lost you feel, God is as close as your breath, or a flash of awareness, or a fleeting opening of the heart. Anywhere, anytime, stop. Know that the divine creator abides with you in infinite closeness.*

TUNE IN TO RESONANCE

Place yourself in that cave with your own version of an altar. What sacred objects or images would you want to have? Think of carefully setting each one on your altar. Ask for a message that is pertinent for you in the deepest sense of your personal search for direction and meaning. Be open to the answer coming through your practice as you allow presence to touch you in this quiet place of imagination and in this present moment.

How Does Communication with Presence Relate to Healing?

Bear in mind that healing is in one sense ordinary and in another extraordinary. A basic aspect of most organisms, healing is part of life. The processes of renewal are built into our most basic nature. Some would say that deep within our Self (the God-Presence within each of us) we are fundamentally healers. To realize that natural state and to reveal it progressively in action makes it visible as a skill in healing.

For Christians, the third aspect of the Trinity, the Holy Spirit, brings the gift of healing to followers. Of course, the healing ministry of Jesus is a core Christian tenet and intense in its reach. In Judaism, prayers and songs offered for the healing of individuals and of the earth are an established part of daily practice. In Hindu philosophy, healing is one part of a transcendent consciousness attained through practices known as the eight limbs of yoga. Meditation is one of those practices. In Vajrayana Buddhism, advanced meditative practices include precise visualization of specific deities. One also imagines union with the deity. The outcome of these traditional practices is a natural expression of the qualities of integrity, compassion, and loving regard for others.

In aboriginal cultures, shamanic healing is an integral part of life. Certain members of the tribe are identified, chosen, and trained as healers. In the Kung tribe of Africa, dance is the method of developing spiritual energy and the dancer/healer "begins to *kia,* or experience an enhancement of their consciousness."[5] The altered state achieved in such acts is considered by the Kung to be a growth of consciousness. A healer develops skill through repeated experiences that are accurately identified as transcendent. As seen dramatically in the Kung dances, one of the attributes we have as humans is to expand our consciousness and thereby transcend the limits of ordinary reality.

In Bali, healers, referred to locally as *balians*, can come to their vocation through two routes. They may be born into a family with an established balian and receive the transmission of the lineage through special ceremonies. Once identified as a balian, the person dedicates his or her life to serving others as a trance medium, a physical touch healer, or deep touch practitioner. The deep touch is similar to pressure point or acupressure therapy, and can be initially quite painful. When I received this type of work not only were thumbs pressing way into my muscles, the balian walked on my back. After three days of bruises and hobbling around, I felt terrific.

The other path to become a balian is through a deathlike experience. The first Balinese healer I worked with, Jero Tapakan, was so ill that her family was grieving her demise. She was right at the doorway of death when she woke and found a weeping throng around her. Unlike Westerners who routinely describe their near-death experiences as starting with a passage down a long, dark tunnel with light at the end, Jero Tapakan's image was of walking in a dense forest on a trail that led to a crossroads where a tribunal was waiting for her. Four "siblings" showed up and plead her case. The Balinese believe that each person comes into the world with four sibling helpers. Those four are spirit beings. In her vision, she agreed to dedicate herself to be a healer, a calling she had previously shunned. After her surprisingly rapid recovery, she met with a local balian who confirmed that her vocation was authentic. The community then fully embraced her. Jero Tapakan was a trance medium, a massage therapist in the deep acupressure style, and maker of healing potions. She told me that she would go to the jungle and collect vines and other vegetation as she was instructed by impressions from those she named as angels or guides. She mashed the gathered materials and mixed them thoroughly using a mortar and pestle. Then she stirred *arak*, a potent rice wine, into the mash and gave the slurry to the ill person to drink. Many potions were made specifically for that individual. Jero Tapakan also told me that sometimes it was the job of the healer to take the slurry into her mouth and spit it on the bare skin of the sick person. Curiously, this technique was also used by Mayan healers long ago.

She became one of Bali's best-known healers. Her techniques were given to her in trance through her guides. She claimed that she could ask her god a question, and her god could communicate with the patient's god and tell her what to do.

Communication happens mysteriously—in meditation, in transcendent states of consciousness, and through guidance from unseen sources. The transcendent states, although temporary, lastingly change us.

TUNE IN TO RESONANCE

Using the following poem, consider your roles both as a person who wants to heal and as one who wishes to assist others in healing.

Are you called to heal?
How much courage do you have?
Can you hold focus, and hold, and hold it?
Can you let the outcome be whatever it is?
Are you called to heal?
Have you discovered how to be safe?
Can you penetrate illusion?
The good, better, and best facade?
Did you decide to be a healer?
That might trap you.
Do not decide, rather follow.
Do not conjure, simply respond.
Remember the Presence.
Remain in the Presence.

The World of the Subtle Senses

When we discuss presence and communication, we quickly enter a dimension that is both tangible and mysterious. This is a situation that cannot be captured by any physicist's equation. Anyone who has authentically felt the presence is convinced that it is not imagination, wishful thinking, nor psychosis. When I was a child, I experienced the mystery of the subtle senses in many ways. My father would often arrive home from his long day at work after I had been tucked into bed by my mother. My bedroom window faced the driveway. I would hear his car approach the garage right outside my window. I stood on my bed and looked out, but the driveway would be empty. I learned to stay there quietly. Within two or three minutes his car would groan up the steep crest of the driveway, and rumble to the flat part where I could see it glide into the garage. I never thought about the curious time lag between when I first heard his car engine and when he actually arrived. As a kid, I thought it was just the way it was. Didn't this happen to everyone? The communication of my father's impending arrival was 100 percent accurate. Whatever subtle sense picked this up touched my auditory centers so that I "heard" him before he was actually there. In Nordic countries this phenomenon is called "the Doppelganger effect." Many wives rely on it to know when to start dinner.

Herein is a key to connection with presence: knowing what subtle senses in us inform our ordinary sensory system. Sometimes a divine fragrance is experienced. Devotees of Mother Mary often report the fragrance of roses in a cathedral or other sacred site. For some an image of a peaceful place or a safe place such as a secure garden provides a sanctuary sufficient for deep meditation and for the subtle presence to be experienced. The sound of soothing music, devotional chanting, or one's own voice repeating a mantra opens the gateway to that peaceful altered state of mind where presence can communicate with us. It is not uncommon for those who repeat mantras to at some point "hear" the mantra being repeated within. Others may hear subtle strains of music or chanting. In this way our outer spiritual practices awaken us to the inner realms and allow us to go deeper into the experience of presence. This deepening feels something like shifting from one state of consciousness to another. It seems that we work in several dimensions. There is a natural arc from our cells to our brain that informs us of many of the needs of our body: time for lunch, get your hand away from the flame, time to sleep, pay attention to that pain in your knee. These flow from the unseen world of our cells to the knowable. Yet another arc loops from subtle perception to the mystery of the spiritual dimension. Yearning for spiritual communication is universally human but lacks an absolute answer. Because we can't explain it does not mean that it is unattainable. The good news is that the yearning for that contact with presence opens the door to practices that you can adapt in your own best way.

THE PRACTICE: PRESENCE AND COMMUNICATION

In Bali a temple is considered to be nothing more or less than a beautifully constructed edifice until people gather for a ceremony. Hundreds of colorfully attired men, women, and children arrive with baskets of offerings piled high. Music begins—the music of gongs, gamelan, and chant fill the air. Incense is burned in massive amounts. The air is fragrant with the rising smoke of bundles of incense sticks. The Balinese believe that God notices the rising incense and sends blessings back down through the smoke to the people. We can borrow from this image for a practice to open our senses and invite the experience of presence and communication.

Allow the focus of your attention to rest in your heart space. Visualize a whiff of sweet fragrance of devotion rising from the center of your heart to the Universe or God as you know that presence. Spend a few minutes expanding your own yearning for communication with that presence. Imagine your desire for that connection to float up from you as a cloud of incense.

Allow a sense of blessing, a conscious awareness of it, to travel back down the sweet smoke to your heart. The flow upward from you and the flow back to you create connection. Let that connection become a conduit for communication and guidance.

Envision the energy coming to you as a nourishing flow that moves throughout your body, transmitting life and healing into every cell.

CHAPTER 4

CONNECTION AND PROTECTION

Be empty of worrying
Think who created thought!
Why do you stay in prison
when the door is so wide open?
Move outside the tangle of fear-thinking.

— R U M I

The morning was overcast, the air softly humid and spiced with hints of incense. Balinese storekeepers emerged with sleepy eyes to place tiny baskets on the bottom step of their storefronts. Each basket was hand-woven and carefully adorned with flower blossoms. Burning sticks of incense were stuck in the side of the basket and supported by the weave of the grasses that an older family member had made. Fragrance blessed the air.

These offerings dotted every place of business, every tiny shop along Monkey Forest Road, the main street for cafés and stores in the mountain town of Ubud, in the central part of the tiny island of Bali. This was my third trip, and future returns would stretch into a ten-year commitment to train with Jero Mangku Srikandi, a Balinese shaman-healer, a *balian* in her language. I had met another master healer, Jero Tapakan, on an earlier excursion to Bali, and was blessed by her insights, but decided to work exclusively with Jero Mangku. This honored the Balinese way of training with one master healer and only one. I realized that the invitation to study with Jero Mangku was rare for a Westerner and required a wholehearted dedication from both of us. I had no idea at the time that we would continue from 1990 through 2000. What ended the training was Jero's declaration that I had passed all the appropriate tests and initiations and was a balian by Balinese standards.

On this particular morning, however, I was in the tourist area of Ubud, strolling at dawn's first light to see the rituals that shopkeepers make before their stores open and long before jet-lagged tourists wander out from their hotels to browse carvings, fabrics, and other crafts displayed along the half mile of road. I had been in Bali for several weeks. My biological clock was reasonably reset, and I found myself up with the roosters who robustly heralded each morning. As I wandered down the road, enjoying a relaxed morning, I responded to something that made me stand up very straight. I came to an alert awareness. Looking around for the source of the strange feeling, I saw a person walking toward me from the direction of the forest. As the figure approached, I saw a man who was distinctly dressed in black. That alone was unusual for Balinese men.

Considerably more unusual was the odor that accompanied him, like a personal cloud. It was not sweaty body odor or something fetid. It was hard to identify. The smell was immediately strange, and not one I wanted to keep inhaling. Intuitively, I wanted to avoid him—to find an open shop and duck inside—but nothing was open, and there were no buffers that a crowded street would have provided later in the day.

My relief was tangible as we passed each other without incident, and I was alone again walking rapidly in the opposite direction. I had no desire to look back, only a forward impetus to put as much distance between us as I could. The rest of the morning was as relaxed and pleasant as usual in the splendor of Bali, and I forgot about the darkly clad man. Once again, I became absorbed in the sounds of chanting and the lovely smell of incense that the morning blessing rituals provided.

Shopkeepers as well as householders made two kinds of offerings upon waking. One is placed in a beautifully carved tray and is placed high up. Fresh flowers, grains of rice, and several sticks of incense grace these small shrines. Prayers are said as the properly clad shopkeepers face the shrine. By properly clad, I mean that a sarong, temple scarf, and colorful shirt or blouse are worn. For men, a special hat, somewhat the shape of a sailor's hat, is perched on the head. Women wear their inky black hair long and shiny, well brushed and adorned with fragrant plumeria flowers. Most often a small statue of one of the Hindu deities resides on a ledge above the offering.

The second type of morning offering is those cup-sized baskets I had seen on my early-morning walk. Along with incense and flowers, these contain rice and possibly bits of crackers or other small pieces of food. The Balinese believe that should there be a malicious spirit touring the street, it would be better to feed it, rather than have it come up the stairs and enter the shop to make mischief. The Balinese way is to not fight when conflict can be avoided, especially when something as simple a small basket of rice and crackers could appease a bad spirit. Protection for the shop and the shopkeeper is, therefore, a simple daily activity to which everyone adheres. Another traditional offering for protection is a piece of banana leaf adorned with rice, salt, grated coconut, and turmeric. This offering is also placed on the ground near homes and places of business. Since banana trees are not always plentiful in the center of town, woven baskets are used as a serving vessel.

TUNE IN TO RESONANCE

Visualize yourself in a beautiful place. You hold a small woven basket in your hands. Mindfully place a few simple things in your basket—a slice of apple, a walnut, a symbol of your spiritual connection such as a cross, a pendant, or a picture of your guru. Let each item remind you that you are safe in the deepest parts of yourself where you dwell in union with the creator. This is a practice you could physically do as you place items on your own altar or simply on a cloth.

My subsequent morning strolls were blissfully uneventful as I enjoyed the fragrance of the morning offerings and the quiet of Monkey Forest Road. Days after the initial incident, I took two students who had accompanied me to Bali on a visit to Goa Gajah, the Elephant Cave, a large temple complex with pools, fountains, and a famous cave. The grounds of the complex were beautiful. There were steps leading down to pools of clear water with a stone statue at one end of each of the six pools.

Upon entering the temple grounds, one was expected to remove his or her shoes, descend the steps to the water's edge, and purify oneself by splashing this sacred water on head, hands, and shoulders. Local wisdom claims that the water from each of the six statues has healing power for different conditions. One for infertility, one for arthritis, and so on. This is a holy, peaceful, and healing place with no hint of negative energy.

The main attraction was the hillside a few yards from the bathing pools. This rock outcropping was elaborately and deeply carved with myriad images. Dwarfed by the immensity of the hillside was an opening into a cave. Even this was carved so that it appeared you were walking into the mouth of a giant woman with huge, bulging eyes, and drooping earlobes adorned with earrings. The inside was T-shaped with right and left passageways. Niches in the inner rock lined the passages, and at the end of each was a special shrine with sacred objects. The chin-high niches were only large enough for someone to sit cross-legged. Sages of long past had used these as meditation cells for years on end to enter deep solitude. The cave was now a tourist attraction, but it maintained a sacred feeling and a hush. Without signs requiring silence, no one spoke at all, or at least louder than a soft whisper. Perhaps the meditating sages left an aura of peace, an essence of bliss, and an unnamed presence that prompted quiet respect.

The three of us emerged from the mouth of the cave, spit back out into the bright sun of a warm Bali day from the giant's mouth. We walked to an open-air but covered area and sat on a bench to enjoy our personal musings. After a few minutes of relaxing, I got a whiff of that strange odor, exactly the same as from the man I had encountered on Monkey Forest Road days before. Then he appeared, seemingly, out of nowhere, and walked directly toward us. How could he be here in the midst of such sacred energy and peace? I watched incredulously as he grabbed one of the ever-present ducks that wander around such temples. His hand was clenched around its neck. Its feet dangled in the air. The duck's eyes were wild with fear. The man looked directly at me, and I got the impression that he was about to kill the duck right before our eyes. As I caught my breath, I spoke to him from my mind without audible words: *Put the duck down. Do not harm it. Leave now. There are no other options. Do as I say now.* I had no fear, no doubt, and absolute resolve. In fact, he immediately put the duck back on the ground unharmed, turned around, and left the temple grounds. A wave of relief washed over me, followed by a second wave of surprise at my uncharacteristic "in-your-face," yet utterly silent, course of action. Upon later reflection, I noted that my internally voiced English commands were appropriately translated into this man's understanding.

Although Bali is a place of great beauty and spiritual depth, there is a confusing mix of sorcery in the midst of the purity of divine blessing and love. I learned more about the quality of discernment there than in any other of my wanderings, as I sought teachers to further my work as a healer. Sensitivity to the energies around me has become more and more important in everyday life. In Western culture we do not create offering baskets, nor do we expect to encounter mystical forces. Yet is not uncommon in our lives to encounter people who are unsettled and unsettling, whose grasp of reality is shaky, or even pathological. How can we maintain the kind of balance that allows for both openness and safety in our lives? Perhaps we can benefit by taking a page from Balinese culture—by visualizing an offering from our hearts to the heart of God and asking for grace and for that relaxed awareness that works best for us. To be confident within yourself and know that you are safe in this universe and that the connection to spirit creates safety, however we name that presence, is of great value.

Could it be that the protection of God's love or presence abides with us at all times and in all places regardless of circumstances? When the windshield cracks, the roof leaks, a fall on the ice breaks a hip, or cancer strikes, is it possible that the message is not that we have done something wrong, and presence is punishing us? In my experience, at these times we have simply entered the mystery of suffering. The why is often unknown. There is protection in this zone of suffering, just as there is inner strength when creepy sorcerers threaten. Although "stuff" may happen in everyone's lives, we are never alone. Our connection to the abiding love of God is not a talisman against calamity, but it is our truest protection, even when we find ourselves in the "valley of the shadow of death."

Curious Phenomena

Spiritual awakening is often accompanied by unexpected phenomena. The seeker closes her eyes and sees luminous colors of purple, blue, and gold; or curious shapes, even faces that float in and out of the inner visual field. The colors come unbidden and, for some, remain visible with open eyes. Other strange images or voices may arise spontaneously. Religious traditions from Hinduism to mystical Christianity have identified such phenomena as part of an expanding spiritual experience.

Current research in brain function shows intriguing shifts in brain-wave frequency during altered states of consciousness. These states are entered chiefly through meditation. They occur along with images or colors, and often while the person being tested is praying for another's healing or well-being.[1]

For many Westerners, phenomena of this type are frightening, particularly because we have no precedent for them in our culture. The more than 12 million near-death experiencers in the United States are part of the growing number who find themselves puzzled or scared by such visions. I was teaching a workshop at Omega Institute in New York when one of the participants, Toby, slumped over and loudly proclaimed, "I'm seeing purple: bright purple with my eyes open or closed." He continued, "I hate this. I want it to stop."

Toby is a bright, talented designer and a world traveler. His rational world seemed to crumble with this onset of what appeared to be a spontaneous spiritual awakening. He became a private client of mine, and we worked together via telephone between his East Coast home and my Seattle office. The core issue was safety. He felt vulnerable, his world shaken, if not turned upside down. Our work was to help him establish a firm spiritual connection and an understanding that the phenomena were a classic blessing, a natural inner state. He wanted to feel safe and sought protection that, up until then, had eluded him.

There is a pricelessness in the lived experience of protection through pure connection with Spirit, God, the Universe—however you may name the Source. My work with Toby started my own personal reflection on how I found a secure sense of safety in the midst of any number of strange happenings. In the early days of my own spiritual development, I journeyed to the Philippines and to Bali to explore what native healers knew about consciousness and how to focus prayer or energy for healing. I was tested time after time and challenged repeatedly by my teachers. As the result of years of work with them, and through the practices I pursued, I found a connection to Self that continually deepens my sense of spiritual union.

TUNE IN TO RESONANCE

Reflect on your own sense of where you are most at one with Self and Source. How does breath work to take you to a deep place inside? What image or words or songs propel you there? When silence comes to you, relax into it. Allow yourself to experience the essence of "Be still and know that I am God."

There have been a number of occasions for me to learn the abiding nature of God and to explore the principles of the connection–protection couplet. One lesson came with a series of ceremonial tests on one of my trips to Bali to work with my primary master teacher, Jero Mangku Srikandi.

Jero Mangku tested the solidity of my connection to Self and to the Universe during this stay. I was invited to a ceremony to be tested and, as requested, arrived early in the morning at Jero Mangku's home. (Jero is a general title for a master healer, and I will refer to Jero Mangku as Jero from hereafter.) She lived within a typical Balinese complex of small cottages, which had a central garden, open-air sitting area, cluster of small family temples, and Jero's sacred shrine room. Jero emerged from her cottage perfectly and properly dressed for the ceremony in a white lace top, white sarong, and wide red temple sash. Stacks of offerings were ready to be stored in the trunk of the car. Our entourage included three elderly ladies, also bedecked in temple garb, and Jero's husband, dressed in his priestly garments. As instructed in detail by Jero, I was attired in a blue plaid sarong and red temple blouse with a dark blue sash tied around my waist. This attire had been specified by Jero for our visit to the Mother temple, Besakih, a cluster perched 3,000 feet up on the slopes of Mount Agung. The holy mountain rises some 10,000 feet in northeast Bali. We hustled into two cars and headed out for the two-hour trip to the mountain. As we left the bustle of the city where Jero lived, and the car traversed the windy road to Mount Agung, the air became clear and clean, and the rice fields yielded to steep slopes of exotic fruit trees and wild jungle vegetation.

We arrived at the outskirts of the Besakih complex, zipped around a guard station, and stopped behind a small temple that formed an entrance to the enormous temple grounds. Jero got out, grabbed my hand, and ushered me through the back gate of this small temple, which brimmed with women and men preparing offerings and food for an upcoming celebration. Only a dog or two seemed to notice my foreign intrusion as they perked up their ears and issued a perfunctory bark or two. We walked through the busy outer temple and approached the gate into the main Shiva temple at the center of Besakih.

We trooped in on the finishing prayers of a purification ceremony for a large family just completing the death rites of a cremated family member. Minutes after the priest finished his blessings, a few drops splashed out of the clouds, then more followed until a downpour drove us under the thatched shelters directly in front of a central Shiva shrine. Jero discoursed with five priests, the resident clergy who would decide if our ceremony could proceed. The priest in charge for this day was a woman with two men and two women assistants. Women have many positions of responsibility in the network of sacred activities in Bali. Jero was assisted by her husband, who is also a priest, though not a balian. The conference seemed to go on and on. Jero spoke quietly and forcefully in one of the five Balinese dialects: the one reserved solely for sacred ceremonies and sacred conversations. She had the full attention of the other priests. They responded only briefly and everyone flashed beaming smiles. She gestured toward me, waved me to the shelter where the meeting had been, and I knelt there with her and my translator to hear the decision. More waiting! Could anything move this along? Had the priests approved Jero's request? What did their smiles actually signify? I was so jittery.

TUNE IN TO RESONANCE

Recall a situation when you had to wait to know what was to happen next. Perhaps that is an everyday occurrence! Rest into a state of anticipation with alert attention but without anxiety. Your breath can help you release tension as you wait. Take several deep breaths and welcome the next moment, the next email, the next instruction from your supervisor, or the next thought you have for how to proceed with your day.

Jero began a chant. The priests had approved the request. What timing—the rain suddenly stopped and sunshine burst out along with an inspirational view of Mount Agung. The mountain seemed to rise up in front of us as if it were newly formed. Jero pulled me up from my seated position and out into the open space in front of the Shiva shrine. She wanted me to sit down on the wet ground, and, of course, I complied. I sat cross-legged in the smallest puddle I could locate. The warmth and humidity of the air made this a sort of total immersion as if floating in warm water. Comfortable or not, I had no time to be miserable as my attention was drawn to Jero as she stood above me and positioned her arms as in a traditional sacred dance. Her eyes grew fierce, and she began to move around me. Her voice boomed a chant, and she bumped against me. Whack. Her hip smacked me on one side and then the other as she moved around. She lashed at me with wet flowers and leaves. She stopped and told me to open my mind, then asked what I saw.

"I see gold all around, streaming up from the earth and down from the sky. I see purple colors and lightning bolts of energy along with the gold." As surprising as that was, it was as tangible an experience as I have ever had or hope to have, and it remains as vivid for me today as it was all those years ago.

The dance and chants began again. Jero's ferocity increased. She drew herself way above me and darted down to my face. She looked as if she would devour and destroy me. I was surprised at my lack of fear and lack of reactivity to her whacks. I had no desire except to be right there. There was a feeling of great power surging through my body and my hands came up from my lap and began to shake. The shaking continued strongly. Eventually my whole upper body was shaking violently. Jero was right in front of me with the palms of her hands toward me. The emotion I felt was a curiously neutral sort of ecstasy. Then Jero knelt on my legs with her whole weight and asked me again to relate what I saw.

"I see a giant cobra above your head, Jero. It cloaks you as it dives down from the open sky. My hands are full of fire, a density of energy I have not felt before. The fire extends about two feet out beyond my palms."

My guide and translator, Budi, sat right beside me and he quietly said to me. "Jero had tested you for black magic. If you were using sorcery or had been cursed you would not have shaken as you did. You are fine, free of evil." I was immensely relieved by this message and also grateful that the shaking stopped. I wondered why I signed up for this! In retrospect, I know the cobra vision was a sign of blessing and acceptance, and a transmission of grace.

My thoughts were interrupted by more dancing. Jero placed flowers on me. Some were on my head, some tucked inside my shirt, and some were all over me as Jero began to fling them. My hands felt hot with a sensation of pulsing energy. My flesh seemed to thin out into a continuum of pure energy. A vision of a bull's skull with dark eye sockets and horns materialized. The image faded back into the distance and I saw purple and white stars bursting in dance. The stars touched me, and the sensation was wonderfully sweet.

Without fanfare or conversation, the ceremony was over. Jero led us in a closing prayer in the normal Balinese sequence. First, we addressed the empty space of pure mystery, then the sun god, Brahma, Vishnu, and Shiva, the God of our heart, and again to the vast, empty space of God's presence. She anointed us with holy water and poured some into my cupped right hand to drink. Again we were generously sprinkled with holy water splashed from a container onto our heads via the petals of the holy flower, plumeria. We were given tidbits from the offering baskets: bananas and brightly colored rice muffins.

It felt as though I floated from the shrine back to our car. I was ecstatic. The rules of living in my body seemed to have shifted forever. Through this experience, I began to understand that I can touch the deep Self. I can trust that place in me. For each of us there is a true Self, a blessed seed of the most sacred. The connection that comes from the awareness of that Self is gentle, immediate, and safe. I do not need to hope that an amulet, a certain mantra, a specific holy site, a church nave, or anything else affords protection. The connection of Self with the Universe is sufficient.

Before this particular initiation in Bali, meditation was a discipline for me. Afterward it became a time of delight to practice throughout the day. Meditation became as valuable as breathing; in other words, it was life giving and life sustaining. I've found in my own life that the resources of practice which support connection also support patience. Safety follows and also allows room for additional qualities such as compassion and clarity to accompany the journey.

TUNE IN TO RESONANCE

To find connection may require exploring patience, which is not one of my personal best qualities. How about you? Do you also find that time seems to run out when you tick off the items on your agenda? We are so busy. What would you do if a meditative practice became a high priority? Imagine you can set the day's tone with a meditation—even a few minutes of practice. If this is new for you, consider scheduling moments for you to be alone, in silence, to receive blessing. That leads to the experience of connection that always provides protection.

Protection in Everyday Life

In the middle of an island paradise like Bali, after a life-changing ceremony, in the ecstatic presence of a master teacher, everything seems well and good. What about life back home? What about work, groceries, and relationships? How does this relate to our bodies, our cells, and healing?

Our personal experience of protection and connection can begin with the way our body works. Cells are specialized and highly adapted to manage particular areas of vulnerability. Skin cells in humans preserve our outer form and protect us from all sorts of environmental intrusion without being an immovable covering of armor. To do this skin cells produce keratin, a tough, waterproof protein. The cells responsible for making keratin are called keratinocytes. Among other activities, they make alpha keratin, a particular type of helical protein that forms numerous long strands that twine around each other. Not only the internal structure of keratinocytes speaks to resilience, but the cell itself forms tight junctions with nerves in the skin, preserving the integrity of skin structure while providing the delicate sensation of touch. Yet another attribute of keratinocytes is their ability to enlist other cells for protection when needed. They can mount their own form of immune response to a scratch or cut and can also signal a full inflammatory response within the skin structure of the epidermis, dermis, and other subcutaneous components. There are a variety of levels at which these cells protect the body. The internal world of the keratinocytes is a scaffolding of helical fibers that coil up with pressure and spring back when the pressure is released. The fibers are also waterproof and make the whole skin surface water resistant. Just think what it would be like if your skin were more like a sponge—if it soaked up all the shower water, bath water, or spring rain falling on your head.

The next level of connection in keratinocytes is their contact with nerve cells. The tight junctions they form allow skin to experience touch in its many forms without tearing or damage to the tender nerves that interlace between the keratin-making cells. Because the helical fibers of keratin can compress and bounce back, the skin does not tear or puncture easily. However, when something does penetrate, skin cells can immediately produce substances that are part of the immune system's first line of defense to prevent infection. With enough of a wound, keratinocytes have the capacity to create considerable inflammation that signals far-flung regions of the body to send additional immune system cells to the site of invasion and initiate a thorough healing response. This response includes cells that handle invasive organisms such as bacteria and cells that begin repair of the structural damage. In essence this is like a call to 911, which brings aid to us in times of difficulty.

The parallel lessons of keratinocytes with a more general sense of connection and protection speak to the resilience of each of us as individuals. We each have our own sense of self, developed in a variety of ways, and ranging from shaky to solid. That is the first line of protection. Then we are connected in close proximity to a local community of people—our family, our "beloveds," our friends, and everyone else we interact with directly. Beyond this network are the public protectors: firefighters, police, and government.

There are times when our best efforts to remain connected are challenged and uncertainty creeps in.

What is to be done then? I learned some of this from my teacher, a healer named Roberto Pidal, in the Philippines. I had studied with him for three months in Baguio, a town in the mountains about six hours by bus from Manila. When I returned to Seattle, I sponsored him and his wife to join me. Each night after we worked together, and he went to his own lodging, I would meditate for a good hour before retiring to sleep. One night in my healing room during a deep meditation, I felt a huge negative energy enter the room and its iciness scared me. It seemed to approach closer and closer. The more I struggled and thought I was fighting it off, the stronger it became. I was increasingly agitated and headed into terror. Roberto's previous admonitions to ignore such "illusions," keep praying, and stay centered in God were very hard to follow. Was the icy presence an illusion? It could have been, but it seemed utterly real. I did follow my teacher's instructions, however, and the fear gradually dissolved, the negativity vanished.

No more icy apparitions showed up, but another astonishing incident showed me the remarkable variety of altered states of awareness. The walk-in basement of my home was a healing space that clients could enter from double doors that opened onto a patio in the backyard. Curtains gave privacy between the part of the room where chairs provided a waiting place and the treatment table, altar, and candles that illuminated the inner room—a quiet healing space. One evening when my family was asleep upstairs and the healing space was empty and still, I sat down to meditate in front of the altar. I pulled a blanket around me and lay down in the inner healing room, and began to feel drowsy. Indeed, I drifted off to sleep. About midnight I was startled by a loud thumping noise, I opened my eyes, still in a half-sleep state. My eyes were drawn to the curtain leading into the healing room. Near the bottom edge a large black spider walked down the curtain. Every movement of each of the eight legs made a sound that pounded like thunder in my head. I was literally hearing the spider descend down the cloth.

As a rational person with a penchant for a scientific approach to life, this was a baffling and bewildering experience. But it was clear to me that this was in fact a demonstration of the way in which altered states of mind also affect our five senses. Such rare occurrences reveal to us the vastness of the universe with which we have little contact or knowledge. I was graced by this noisy spider in my healing space. Enhanced perception of sounds that otherwise would be inaudible is one of the classic signs of expanded consciousness. At a biological level, something dramatic must change in the ear or in the auditory neurons of the brain to hear a spider's footfalls.

Beyond simply boggling my mind, the spider was part of an emerging awareness that we are all one at the deepest level of existence and that our ordinary perception can just open up, as mine did, to reveal that connection. Union is a reality and our connection with God is, indeed, a safe place that leads us to communion with all that is. The mystery of this awareness does not save me from scary moments totally, but it opens many lovely opportunities to bond with other people, animals, and nature that I might otherwise miss.

Substantive spiritual connection involves developing awareness of one's own central core and confidence in one's own true nature as a spiritual being. Almost always, the answers and insights we seek are not conceptual. In other words, we cannot think our way into those answers. As a scientist, with years of developed skill in cognitive approaches to everything, I found this baffling, frustrating, and foolish. It took a long time to trust that guidance and protection were all around me and that I could move into just the right place, just the right connection, without having to rationalize every step and nuance.

Let's return to the wisdom of biology for an example of how oneness is reflected in cell structure and function. Tiny fibers of actin and strands of microtubules streak from one side of a cell to another. This forms scaffolding on which other subcellular parts can have a foothold. Another part of the cell, the folded membranes of the endoplasmic reticulum (See Appendix: Action) reside close to the nucleus. Information carried by molecules made inside the nucleus exit through nuclear pores and hook up with the endoplasmic reticulum, coding for the specific sequence of the protein the cell needs. Those proteins are the enzymes and structural parts of the cell that support the processes that keep us alive. The power packs of the cell, the mitochondria, were once thought to float about the cell. However, recent research shows that there is a molecular cluster that forms a connection between mitochondria and adjacent endoplasmic reticulum, thus ensuring a source of energy required for the synthesis under way.[2] These intricate and submicroscopic connections also ensure the safety of cells—and therefore the life of the body. The principles of connection and protection are demonstrated at every level of being.

THE PRACTICE: CONNECTION AND PROTECTION

This meditation is intended to help you to create an environment in your consciousness where deep connection with Self and with Spirit can provide safety.

Imagine that you enter a sacred cave—the cave of your heart. Allow your heart to be open and full of longing for union with Spirit. Your heart cave can resonate for you as a place that constitutes a "world in itself" or a "universe in miniature."

Fully focus your attention on your heart and imagine a slowly spinning sphere of light surrounding it. Let this represent the connection of your spirituality and Self. Give it a minute or two to become comfortable and tangible. Then imagine that the sphere expands to touch your throat and your solar plexus, keeping the center at your heart. After a bit, expand the sphere once again to touch your forehead and your belly button. Expand even more to touch the crown of your head and the base of your pelvis. With your heart at the center you've now integrated the classic energy centers of the body: communication (throat) and power (solar plexus), insight (forehead) and emotions (navel), your spiritual center (crown of head), and survival in the body (base of pelvis). As you maintain the sphere centered at your heart, let it expand into an ellipse in which your entire body floats in perfect safety and peace, surrounded by light and blessing.

Now pull the ellipse back to a sphere that touches the crown of your head and your pelvis and slowly bring the sphere back to encircling your heart. Rest a moment in the awareness that your Self and Spirit reside there in bliss, connection and with vital protection.

CHAPTER 5

BALANCE AND HARMONY

Happiness is not a matter of intensity but of balance and order and rhythm and harmony.

— THOMAS MERTON

How did we begin? As remarkable as it may seem, these solid-appearing bodies we work, sleep, and play in are made of star stuff. About 40 percent of the larger atoms in your body, such as carbon and oxygen, came from the dust generated by the supernova explosions of stars. The other 60 percent of atoms in your body are hydrogen atoms that formed during the big bang.[1] The legacy of life in the most fundamental sense emerged from monumental explosions. Stardust flew from these cauldrons of creation to the far reaches of the universe where atoms cooled, collided, and stuck together. Either by the most unlikely accident or through a steadfast inner consciousness of creation, the collisions made molecules that now are the basis of all life forms on our earth.

How long have we been here? Our "Blue Planet," a sparkling gem in the galaxy, formed some 4.5 billion years ago, and a billion years later, life appeared. Although there is disagreement on when human life was established, the latest estimates place our appearance about 2.5 million years ago. These physical selves along with all other life on this planet use carbon as the atomic backbone for biological molecules, with oxygen and hydrogen completing 99 percent of all the atoms in our body. Traces of other atoms such as iron, zinc, calcium, and even uranium are part of the constellation of atoms in the additional one percent, but our exquisite complexity generates from only three basic atoms. Those atoms form molecules, and an enormous variety of combinations of molecules form cells. Billions of years ago cells could not only survive, but replicate, and all life proceeded from the original cells. In essence, our history extends back 3.5 billion years.

All the materials—the atoms and molecules—within you today have been recycled for billions of years. The explosions of other supernovas sent more atoms spinning through space, some of which may be part of you now. You carry within you the blast stuff of 10 billion years ago. You are a fully integrated part of the universe—the far reaches of the universe reside in you. The body you use for a lifespan is hardly your own—it is a form that your consciousness inhabits, made of beautifully recycled elements from far-off galaxies. Some part of you may have been silt in the ocean which ascended in seaweed, and found its way to you in sushi. The dust that landed as silt may contain atoms from Leonardo da

Vinci, Charlemagne, or even Attila the Hun, and thousands, if not millions of others.

TUNE IN TO RESONANCE

Open your arms wide and welcome the diversity of composition that you are. Ponder what stardust found its way to you to create your unique and glorious body. Whatever state of health you experience today, allow the timeless atoms in your body to respond to a wave of new life. As that life force surges through your body, enjoy a heightened experience of vitality.

From Ovum to 100 Trillion Cells

The body starts from one fertilized ovum, one that is indistinguishable from a fertilized mouse ovum. Why did you grow into a six-foot-tall human body and not a tiny mouse? A small fraction of genetic code that designates "human" made all the difference. Percentage-wise, we are only slightly different in genetic code from all other animals, and as humans we share 99.9 percent of our DNA with each other. Though we may look quite different on the outside, underneath it all we are practically identical. How strange it is that we look at each other as different—sometimes so different that we choose to hate or even harm each other.

At your beginning, an egg cell, cradled in your mother's warm body, made its way to the surface of an ovary and was released, floating briefly before being wafted by the gently waving folds at the top of the fallopian tube connected to the uterus. As we all know, your father's sperm fertilized the egg, its tail vigorously propelling the enclosed packet of crucial genetic material. The ovum would become you—a unique being. Thus set in motion, you divided with astounding speed into a bundle of cells. All these cells were alike. They were all totipotent—potentially able to make a whole new human—as they rolled and tumbled down the fallopian tube toward the uterus. At five days, you were officially an embryo, the first stage of differentiation. Your cluster of cells were no longer able to create a whole new body as you entered the vast balmy womb of your mother, burrowed into the spongy endometrium where you latched onto your mother's blood supply for oxygen and nutrients. You didn't just touch the endometrial surface; your round bundle of cells was able to nest deeply into the soft maternal cells and you tunneled until you hooked up with a rich blood supply. The outer embryonic cells became the placenta and the inner cluster of cells continued to divide into a mass of cells, known as pluripotent cells, which could specialize into the 200 different cell types of your body-to-be.

On cue during this busy time of dividing, the group of cells responded to some internal "music" and began a twisting dance. As part of the wiggling and spinning, small clusters of cells were dropped off in specific locations that eventually became the crucial organs for your body. By the tenth week of development you already had a large number of brain neurons with 250,000 created every minute. And this did not stop until 100 billion neurons occupied your skull.[2] Eyes, such an important access point to the world, were completely developed by week 24. After you were born you continued rapid growth, but the cells of each organ had been committed to their specific function for months.

Specialization and Replication

Once cells establish their place in the body, they are dedicated to a specific location and to specialized work. All this activity runs on the expression of the codes of life, tucked well below the awareness of the conscious mind. If we had to keep ourselves alive by thinking, we'd all be dead.

Not all cells replicate at the same rate. Skin cells—bumped, brushed, and scrubbed—last about two weeks. New cells replace the ones that have served and died. Red blood cells travel the entire circuit of the body in 20 seconds. They roll along the major arteries and slip through tiny capillaries. The wear and tear predisposes them to a life span of 120 days. By the time a blood cell reaches its old age, it has traveled 1,000 miles through the body. In contrast, liver cells do not have a set turnover rate, but respond to injury in the organ with cell division until the proper numbers of cells once again restore a harmonious quantity. Our bones seem so unyielding and stable, but are replaced every ten years. The fastest rate of cell turnover is in the lining of the small intestine. Every five days new cells take up the tasks that move food along and absorb nutrients through their waving fingerlike projections—the microvilli.

Once set, specialization is ardently maintained. The pancreas is nothing but pancreas. The intestines do not decide they would rather be an ear and quit being intestines. In the midst of this dedication to specialized structure there is a process of cell death (apoptosis) that sculpts parts of the body. At one stage during frog development, for example, there is a flood of thyroid hormone, and the response is that the tadpole tail beings to shrink.[3] In a mouse, the distinct digits of the paw are formed by programmed cell death that separates each digit from a featureless nubbin. Herein is another biological dance: the tango of cell growth, cell division, and cell death. Known as the cell cycle, this dance is controlled by at least two distinct enzyme complexes within each cell. Key proteins either activate or deactivate new cell division. Outside the cell, certain other molecular complexes serve as switches for cell division. Each cell responds to many signals for either prompting or inhibiting new division. Highly responsive to other cells, the balance of replication is usually so fine-tuned that organs stay the same basic size with essential cell numbers for efficient function. The system can malfunction, however, and excessive cell divisions result in the condition we know as cancer. The body is out of balance and clearly the harmony of a healthy life is disrupted when the cell cycle malfunctions.

With all the exquisite balance we experience during embryogenesis, the growth of our young body, and healthy function of our adult body, how does imbalance happen? What has gone wrong that takes us into the journey of disease? Have we brought this on? Can we heal and return to balance?

There are no complete answers to such questions. We ponder what jogged our system out of balance and what it will take to restore robust health. Of course, some conditions are clear. If I have used alcohol excessively for years and my liver develops cirrhosis, the physical cause is directly related. Much of the time, however, malfunction is a mystery with glimpses of clarity when we are lucky. There is little solid evidence that negative emotions or mind states directly cause disease, though this has been a popular cultural notion for some time. It's easy to get sidetracked and stuck in the blind alley of "why." *What did I do? If I don't change my thinking, I won't get well.* In my experience this approach does not work. I've talked to many people who were caught up in the belief that they somehow made the illness happen and that they must figure it out in order to get well. They focus exclusively on searching for their error in thinking, they blame themselves, and in so doing they miss the opportunity to immediately direct their energies toward health.

During episodes of illness, remember that your body remains resilient, active with renewal, and vigorous with the processes that keep you alive. Out of the 100 trillion cells, how many do you suppose might be sick during an illness? The fact is, a small fraction of you is caught up in the illness, while the majority of your cells carry on the full function of life. To focus on health rather than on disease can support your successful use of medical treatment along with practices that help you return to balance and harmony.

TUNE IN TO RESONANCE

Think about the cells that are fully healthy and working seamlessly for you at this moment in time. How can you allow them to work more dynamically for you? Imagine that all the resources of your body are heightened in this instant and a fresh sweep of energy is bringing healing to anything deleterious or out of balance within you. Invite that to happen as you use the poem to consider the quality of balance in a natural world that is constantly in motion

In continuous wiggle mode
This Universal dance
Shifts out of balance
Boogie with it

Spin with it
Creation anew in
Every nanosecond

Close to the Bottom Line:
DNA, Repair, and Cell Memory

Although DNA carries the codes for all the complexity of the body, its expression and the timing of its expression—what cells do and when they do it—is rather a mystery. New studies reveal some intriguing details about one of the ways such expression is activated. Mechanisms that alter how DNA works, but not the code itself, are termed epigenetic, or nongenetic, cellular memory. One of the ways that DNA is changed is through methylation—the incorporation of a methyl group onto DNA. Exactly what causes the methylation to occur and how it shifts the expression of DNA remains a mystery. What is additionally curious about this phenomenon is the long-term action of epigenetic changes to cellular memory. They can maintain cell identity for a long time, but are reversible when the right conditions arise.[4]

Epigenetic changes during embryo development create temporary imbalances in each new stage of growth. In fact, imbalance in an embryo is required for cells that are all alike to differentiate into the specialized organs of our bodies. Embryonic cells interact with each other and with their overall environment, and these interactions cause epigenetic changes in cellular memory. Thereby cellular memory participates in the creation of our uniqueness.[5] In your adult body events can also shift gene expression through epigenetic or cellular memory changes. Our cells are thrust out of balance in ways that may harm us or not. What we do know is that static states are not in our best interest. In the best sense your body changes all the time and responds continually to its internal and external environments.

Some caution is important here. The entire story of who we are, and how we feel or think is not controlled by epigenetic influence. Although it is tempting to ascribe all our woes to methylated DNA, our mother, or some misfortune that changed our genetic expression "there is very little evidence in humans that epigenetics connects early life experience to behavioral or health problems later in life."[6] Yet there are those who point to our conscious influence on epigenetics as the singular key to health or disease at any given moment. This is not supported by current research and is not consistent with the overall complexity of the body. In following the popular notion that all we have to do is repeat the right mantra, do the right visualization, or hold the right thought pattern to shift our epigenetics, we are left with a load of self-blame if we end up with less than perfect health. Again, it is not conscious thought that accounts for and manages the myriad life processes that are going on within the body—thought alone does not keep us alive and well.

The Body Handles Damage to DNA

The body is experiencing constant change, tilted off balance by many things in our inner and outer environments. The codes in DNA that regulate cell renewal and repair are also affected by numerous inner and outer events. Accidental damage to DNA happens constantly. There are thousands of random lesions every day in human DNA that are caused by metabolic mishaps, heat, exposure to toxins from the environment, and random radiation. Our DNA has a cadre of repair mechanisms that include more than ten different enzymes that repair specific types of damage and restore the DNA codes to their original sequences. These repair enzymes are actually produced when damage occurs. They are triggered by the problem itself. In other words, imbalance creates the message that prompts the system to reestablish stability and harmony. Though we may not be able to identify the cause of a given illness, how can we support the body's own operating system as it works to restore health? Can we help ourselves return to physical and mental harmony even though we may not be able to create perfect health in every situation we encounter?

How Do We Apply Cell-Level
Healing to Restore Balance?

Health is a dynamic balance that oscillates within a certain sweep, partially controlled by our genes and partially by epigenetics, and, in a major way, by our response to conditions. It is a major task to recognize what you can control and what you cannot, and respond in a reasonable and effective way. Harmony in the body follows naturally when balance is restored.

How we maintain health dances between the predetermined codes of life, our use of intention, and the impact of our surroundings. For example, it is known that loneliness predisposes many to become ill and die early. A group of researchers at the University of Chicago studied the genetic makeup of lonely people and found genetic differences in 200 genes. Many of these genes were ones that respond to damaged cells, crippling one's ability to repair tissue. Some of the genes also involved reduced antibody production, thus inhibiting a person's ability to ward off infection. Chronic inflammation was the clinical result for these genetic and cellular conditions in lonely people. Understanding the complexities of dynamically interacting systems—from large external systems such as humans and their environment, to microscopic internal systems—is one of the expanding frontiers of current biological research. In the interim, there are healing modalities that work in the dimension of spiritual practice for which we have no mechanistic understanding. Those practices touch our cells and engage our minds in the terrain of mystery in ways distinctive to each individual.

Stacy wrote to me about a healing experience she had several years ago during a private healing session. "I took your first three classes and then I scheduled a session with you to address high-grade precancerous cells on my cervix and uterus. We had a second session prior to my surgery. My doctor was determined to do the surgery as scheduled regardless of my hope that I was healed. When she called with the results she was amazed. Going from a high-grade cancer to none was not something she had ever seen.

"I also wanted to share with you something I experienced in that second session. I didn't share it with you at the time because I was still in shock. We had our initial conversation at the beginning of the session and then hung up our phones and started to work. I focused on healing as you had taught me. I worked through the meditations that you went through with us in the first three classes, including the one called balance and harmony. All of a sudden I was completely out of body. I was looking down on my body, and it was completely surrounded by the hands of angels, and my body was glowing with an intense healing energy/light. The feelings I experienced were so intense. I wanted to stay there and feel what I was feeling (intensity is the best word I can find for it) but I was also fighting it thinking this state was not a relaxed or meditative state that I was supposed to be in during my session. It was a crazy logic I was trying to apply to a completely unfamiliar situation. It was an amazing experience. After you called me back at the end of the session and we hung up, I knew that I was healed. One hundred percent healed. So I was a little sad when my doctor was determined to do the surgery, but the procedure itself went fine and the results were the definitive confirmation I hoped for: no cancer."

In Stacy's case, physical health, balance, and harmony in these specific cells returned in an instant. The physical healings that astound us are the instantaneous miracles. We know from many reports that such events do happen. We so want them to come about regularly. What is the key to creating a miracle? I've asked that many times as a facilitator of healing, and wished that it would be standard and repeatable in every healing session. Instantaneous healings are rare. However, progressive and slower healing does occur frequently and is assisted by spiritual practice.

TUNE IN TO RESONANCE

What would be necessary for you to be in perfect balance and harmony in this moment in time? Gather a few thoughts about that first. Now let go into a deeper state of reverie and simply ask for a message from within without any expectation. Take note of what happens, and be aware that the message may come now or sometime later, it may take the form of words or images or an opening of your awareness. Invite the process of healing to go at a pace that is best for you. Perhaps that is a miracle of instantaneous healing. Perhaps the miracle is your own awareness of the ongoing process of healing that is underway right now.

The Role of Harmony

How does harmony connect with balance? A body out of balance is dissonant. The feeling is antsy—apprehensive. "Something is not right!" On the other hand, a disease may be silently present in the body, and there is no sense of disorder. More common, however, is an unexplainable lack of a consistent internal harmony, which has roots in malaise. With a return to health, the body resonates with the accord of well-being. If we were perfectly attuned to the full harmonic of the body, we might know at the onset when any part is out of balance. It would be possible at such an early stage that simple alternative practices could return the body fully to health. This is an intriguing idea and one we can easily practice without avoiding or ignoring regular medical checkups. Over the years, I've learned that when I am overloaded, and not taking particularly good care of myself, a certain muscle in my neck becomes tight. If I override that call to take time off for renewal, my chest becomes congested, and I may be headed toward bronchitis or pneumonia. My most effective strategy has been to stop all the busyness as soon as I become aware of the signal, load up on vitamin C, take a long, hot bath, and catch up on sleep. This platform for renewal gives me an almost tangible sense of harmony. If I've cut short my meditation practice, I also return to my cushion without time restraints. To enjoy a practice of silence, free of the mind-crunching activity of concern for the next event or the next responsibility is healing in and of itself.

To detect dissonance in the body does require neutral listening. By that I mean we must not approach an assessment of our state of physical or mental harmony with anxiety, neediness, or heightened emotional attachment. A relaxed conscious awareness brings the most reliable information. Once it is clear that something is amiss in the body, the search for help is appropriate and may require some perseverance. Oprah Winfrey had a sense that she was ill and, according to her colleague and physician Mehmet Oz, had to "push" her doctors to find the illness. Oprah had a major hormonal shutdown with a thyroid condition that was not quickly picked up by regular testing. Dr. Oz praised her and encouraged the millions who watch these shows to hold steady as they search for assistance, saying, "You know your body. Push your doctors."

TUNE IN TO RESONANCE

Play a bit with simple balance in the physical body. Stand with an easy straight posture with your arms by your sides. Shift your weight back and forth from one foot to the other. Find the place where you feel most comfortable with equal weight on each foot. Consciously offset your balance by either weighting one foot more than the other or by leaning to one side or the other. After each excursion, return to the center place with increasing confidence in your most naturally balanced posture.

Now lie down and shift your body from right to left to again find the most comfortable place of ease and balance in a supine position.

Next step: sit at ease and with excursions forward and back, side to side and several positions of your legs (crossed, extended, bent) find the seated position that is natural and easy for you. Rest into that place.

From your experience of deep quiet and rest, focus your mind with gratitude on your uniqueness. The expression of your DNA as affected by epigenetic events has influenced your cellular memory at many stages of your life. Allow a keen awareness to develop of your individual sense of being. Associate that with your connection to the oneness that links you to all life and consider how that supports perfect balance and perfect harmony within you.

Make note of where unhealthy or unsatisfying patterns shifts your life toward dissonance. Ask for a specific blessing that can move you forward to a new pivot point of balance. In that way you can use the challenges that life brings to find new balance and to seek harmony in the midst of dynamic human conditions.

How Much Time Does It Take to Heal?

The body's timeline or biological time figures in any healing process. Although many of our illnesses have been with us for some time, we often expect instant healing either by pharmaceuticals, surgery, or miracle. Stories abound from many spiritual traditions that speak of instantaneous healing, and though unrecorded there may be many more that took place over time after a healing encounter. Our expectations limit whether we recognize healing when it is at work in us. Subtle changes can build so that one morning we wake free of persistent pain. We hardly notice that the hip is not sore and our stride is steady. The return of balance and harmony to the body follows its own timetable and is often tied to the built-in repair rate of a given cell population.

Application of Balance and Harmony to Specific Conditions

Groups of cells must respond for healing to proceed. That may be 100, 1,000, or 1 million cells, which seem like a lot, but any of these numbers are a small percentage of the 100 trillion cells in the whole body. Each specialized cell group has its own intrinsic rate of repair. We know that nerve cells grow notoriously slowly after injury. I have clients, however, who experience much more rapid healing of nerve-related damage than their physicians anticipate.

Enhanced recovery after surgery has also been noted by those who receive healing energy prior to, during, or shortly after their procedure. We cannot predict the speed at which healing may occur, and a statement about how fast any one of us can heal from any specific malady is likely to be wrong. It is helpful to allow a possibility that the body may respond to a spiritual component that accelerates, stabilizes, and promotes recovery while engaging that elusive quality—patience.

One of the factors that may limit an educated guess about healing time is that we do not know how many systems may be involved. In a condition such as osteoarthritis, there are a number of cell populations affected. The first place to direct healing energy is to the inflammation in the joints. The release of inflammation can give considerable relief from pain along with facilitating blood flow to the area for oxygenation and nutrition. If the arthritis has caused excess calcification, the cells called osteoclasts are the ones with the capacity to restructure the bone calcification by removal of sharp spicules that cause pain and disfiguration. A second group of cells, the osteoblasts, can lay down smooth bone and repair the edges of the joint where there is damage. It is not necessary to precisely imagine each cell doing its work or to be concerned about the exact sequence of cellular activity in your visualizations, but the closer you can come to the natural way the body heals, the better. This is in contrast to simply praying, "Oh, God. Fix my arthritis." I've not found that approach to be very helpful.

When inflammation is rampant through the body, there is a serious general imbalance. As a precursor for any number of illnesses, including heart disease, inflammation is a condition that is important to reverse and thereby restore essential balance to the body. Diet and exercise are helpful as is spiritual practice to flush out the inflammation, reduce overall stress, and release what may be held as tension. The return to balance in such situations can be felt in an overall sense of well-being before specific physical symptoms improve. Partly an issue of timing, the restoration of harmony follows the biological nature of the cells that do the work.

Cancer can be understood as a major disease in which cells lose balance and harmony. Earlier in this chapter we visited the concepts of cellular memory and how changes as simple as the addition of a methyl group to DNA can alter its expression in cells. In rare cases when damage to DNA is not repaired by the enzymes whose genius is to return the DNA strand to its pristine glory, that gene may send the cell off on a binge of rapid growth that becomes a cancer. Out of balance and causing severe disharmony in the body, cancer may respond to the consciousness of this particular couplet with a return to normal cell division and cell cycle timing. Sometimes that response includes the disappearance of the tumor. Stacy's experience of healing was one in which she had an intense spiritual and visionary incident that instantaneously reset the balance of her body. Much as we would all love to have a similarly spectacular healing event, there is no way to manipulate such an occurrence. It is a gift and an awe-inspiring event.

The practice of balance and harmony may, in fact, be a precursor for such an extraordinary experience and of significant help even when the process is not as spectacular. It is an excellent practice that supports whatever pace of healing is for the highest good. To appreciate the great complexity among the interactive components that influence cellular health is part of effective application of this couplet to any disease state. There are many cell types involved in cancer, for example. In some types of tumors, fibroblasts are recruited and form a protective bundle around the tumor. This makes it difficult for medication to reach the tumor and for the body's own immune system to fully function against it. There are specific enzymes, such as p53, that are known to affect cell division rates and a host of recently discovered cell-level activities that can affect cancer. If all the precise molecular factors were known to medical science, a cure would follow. Research pursues filling in such gaps in knowledge. What, then can we do to help ourselves, if cancer is diagnosed?

The first step is to explore all that medical science has to offer. Next, you can develop ways to not just endure the course of treatment you have chosen, but to work with it for your benefit. Although chemotherapy and radiation are long and arduous and have challenging side effects, there are ways to welcome the infusion, for example, to your body to do the best work for your highest good. Otherwise, the stress of not wanting chemotherapy and proceeding anyway sets up an inner conflict that makes every pill and every treatment a struggle. In decades of working with people in this situation, I've found that a practice of blessing the treatment, including the treatment room, the medical staff, the pharmaceuticals—all aspects of treatment—helps reduce side-effects and promote effective healing. The body is better able to accept the treatment and return to balance, the mind is more at ease.

May the practices of this couplet support your health in every way.

THE PRACTICE: BALANCE AND HARMONY

Breathe in the universal quality of balance as if you could embrace a perfect personal balance for this moment in time. Savor the fullness of your chest, the expansion of your ribs, and the gift of breath.

Allow anything that is dissonant within you, whether you are aware of the details or just have an unsettled feeling, to transform as you hold your full breath for a short pause. Rather than release negativity through your out-breath, give your blessing for transformation to happen in that moment.

Breathe out with the intention to bathe your body with the universal quality of harmony. As you repeat this cycle a number of times, you can extend the flow of harmony to your loved ones, your neighborhood, your town, your nation, and the entire planet.

Breathe in balance. Allow instantaneous transformation. Breathe out harmony.

CHAPTER 6

COMPASSION AND CLARITY

*Your vision will become clear only
when you look into your heart*

— CARL JUNG

*As you live deeper in the heart, the mirror gets
clearer and cleaner.*

— RUMI

I was behind the wheel of my old blue VW Dasher, grinding gears as I drove to my final exam with a healing teacher I had studied with for three years. If I could pass this exam, I would have his endorsement along with an extraordinary sense of accomplishment. He had passed a mere four students in ten years of teaching scores of aspiring healers. I was wound up inside my own thoughts, worries, and anxieties. I had no idea what the test would be, what I was expected to know or do. I did have the information that it was a practical exam, and I would be asked to demonstrate a full healing session on some unknown subject.

Preoccupation and worry captured my mind. *What would I have to do? Who would be there? Was I prepared? Did I know anything about what I was doing?* As a graduate student in both zoology and biophysics, I had been through many written tests, been evaluated on peer presentations, and managed to defend my dissertation as a doctoral candidate. All these I passed more than sufficiently, and I had known to some extent what to expect on those tests.

This one seemed far more elusive. I could not prepare by studying a book or a manual. A few blocks from my teacher's office, I slowed for a yellow light and stopped when it turned red. From nowhere a man on a creeper like the kind garage mechanics use, slid out into the crosswalk. If this guy had any legs, they were not visible in the gnarled heap on top of the flat surface. He propelled himself across the street pushing vigorously with his fisted hands clutched in grimy gloves. The effort it took to make each measured sweep of his knuckles must have been considerable based on the grimaces that moved across his face. Seeing him, my worries dissolved. How could I be so absorbed in my own fussing when this person had such difficulty simply crossing the street? At that moment I became as absorbed in empathic compassion for him as I had been in my fretting.

Not only did my worries dissolve, my mind became as clear as crystal. I grasped that the most basic aspect of the work of healing was compassion, not intellectual protocols. Skill would develop as I practiced within the context of compassion. Even with this new insight and temporary ease of concern, the ensuing final exam was one of the most peculiar experiences of my life.

I started up the stairs to my teacher's office with mixed feelings. The anxiety about what would be required and whether I was up to it lingered in the recesses of my mind, as I continued to reel from the impact of the hardship I had just witnessed. With a substantial effort to drop both, I breathed deeply and entered the office in as neutral a state as I could.

My healing teacher, Dennis, was a lanky fellow with feet that seemed too long for his body. He had a mop of inky black hair that never looked combed and an innocent smile radiating from somewhere far beyond his face. He wore the same black pants in every class and every day for his private appointments. Buttoned close to the side of his neck was a brown asymmetric collar, the top of his kurta, which had become his standard attire, a healing uniform that had long sleeves and a mid-thigh-length hem, all of the same dull earth tone in a coarse weave of cotton, almost burlap. All in all, he was just about as odd a fellow as one could find. The other side of that picture was the fact that since he was a young child he had been gifted with healing. With all of his idiosyncrasies, he was an astoundingly fine healer.

As we entered his treatment room, he said to me: "I am going to be your subject on the treatment table. Furthermore, I will go into a deeply altered state and take on illness. I will not be conscious at that point, and will die if you do not work quickly and properly."

Now I was thoroughly afraid. There was no time to quell my fear or bargain with him, as he flopped down on the table the minute he finished his last word and started shaking and twitching. The display looked precisely like a serious seizure. My impulse was to run into the next room, a business office of sorts, grab the telephone, and dial 911. I also had the "Oh, sure" thought but looking at Dennis was most unsettling. He did not look like an actor playing a role for his student. He looked half dead.

I prayed for guidance and started working without a protocol. There was simply none for such a situation. Nothing happened quickly, but I actually could feel a pulse of life, a flow of positive energy where there was none when I began. Slowly Dennis moved a bit. I kept at it. I brought energy down each arm, down each leg, placed my hands on his head and could feel heaviness that I seemed to be able to pull away from him. I worked on his chest by placing my hands directly on his brown shirt, and my focus was to reach any illness or antilife energy around his heart and dissipate it. I moved from one part of his body to another as guided, and as I could feel a rhythm of strength return to what had appeared lifeless. He did come back completely in about an hour; we did not need the paramedics, and I passed the test. To this day I do not know if Dennis was having a grand time acting. He certainly did not indicate that this was anything other than a true state of illness that he had taken on for my test.

What part did compassion play? As I settled into the work at hand with my comatose teacher, the compassion I had felt earlier that morning for the legless man in the crosswalk came strongly to me. The combination of that heartfelt state and the clarity that accompanied it were the qualities that enabled healing. One without the other would result in failure. I have found that the two together are essential for healing work and for many life situations we face. The clarity of compassion opens the gateway of reliable and efficacious guidance. Otherwise we get caught in our own analytical machinations, which generally do not lead to good results or to healing.

TUNE IN TO RESONANCE

How busy is your mind? Imagine that your breath can circulate inside your skull. Each time you breathe in, bring a calm stream of deliciously clear mountain air to the 100 billion neurons in your brain. Each time you breathe out, bathe your being and surroundings with images of peace, brilliant colors, and the fragrance of compassion. All your cells respond to that fragrance with renewed energy and vitality.

Compassion is more than a kindly point of view. It is a quality of mind that shapes our brain. Research has established that certain cells respond to the practice of meditation—specifically to meditation that includes a focus of compassion. Those responding cells are important to our cognitive function: brain neurons increase in number.[1] Simply as an antiaging practice this is good news. Most likely other populations of cells also respond to similar practices, although there is no research to either support or refute this idea at present. Anecdotal evidence from my own and other healers' case studies provide intriguing and hopeful evidence that cells throughout our body respond to compassion and to meditation.

Clarity is manifested in both the mental and physical aspects of our well-being. Mental clarity allows us to organize and integrate the information we receive through our senses. The absence of clarity creates miscues as a result of muddled perceptions and flawed assumptions—all impediments to compassion and to healthy living. We risk the inclination to settle with our projections rather than reach a deeper, true clarity. To stop and allow compassion to catch up, it enables the gift of clarity to emerge. When we are clear about ourselves and about others, our compassion expands naturally.

Identifying True Compassionate Action

How can we distinguish between compassionate action and some other underlying emotion? Martha's story illustrates one aspect of that distinction. Martha's husband, George, died from a heart attack. That heart had sustained him for 56 years, just as it had sustained Martha, their children, their overly green lawn, and their classic bungalow home. George made sure that the plumbing worked, and that the safety gates were in place so no toddler tumbled down the stairs. If the walls had ears they would have heard the joyful melodies of children laughing, happy holidays well spent, and kindness toward one another. Beneath it all were Martha's daily dedicated prayers: "Hail Mary, Full of grace, Blessed art thou . . . " The rosary sustained her. The Catholic mass spoken in Latin calmed her as the years of diaper changes, ear infections, assembly lines of lunch boxes, and teenage rebellions steadily unfolded.

The house was quiet after the children grew up and left to start their own families. She could hear the fourth step to the upper bedrooms squeak a little. Was that sound new? Perhaps they hadn't heard it over the fullness of a family simply doing what families do.

When George died, the formerly gentle quiet grew ominous. Why so untimely a death? Was it because George had neglected his faith? He seldom went to mass once little Angela came along. And after their fourth, there was always something else to do—a tree to prune, a bicycle to fix, a clogged toilet to clear.

When the initial shock of his death lessened, Martha began to fear for his soul. She believed that his goodness was not enough. Her love for him could not tolerate imagining George lost in the shadow realms outside of heaven. Was he damned to wander in darkness? As her mourning took on this new fear, grief filled the bedroom, crept up the stairs, and permeated her thoughts.

One day she decided she knew what to do—ask for a suffering. So she asked, just like that, for an illness—for a suffering that she would carry in order to help George's soul. She would carry the neglect of religious attentiveness for him and hope that through her pain, his soul might find peace—might find God. She was consumed by guilt that she had somehow failed George by not insisting that he come to mass with her and the children.

When she asked for this suffering, she was quickly afflicted with aches and pains; the most debilitating was severe acid reflux. For six long years, Martha suffered. She prayed her rosary daily with mindless speed. Those words no longer had meaning, only the tone and cadence remained while the physical pain overtook her body. In the midst of this misery, Martha called me for an appointment, having heard me on a radio interview. It took two months before I could work with her, as my practice was quite busy. When we did connect, I listened to her story of loss and pain. There was more than resolve in her voice, as she said, "This is enough. I asked to suffer for George's soul and six years is *enough!*"

Our session was via telephone as she lived in South Dakota. After our initial conversation, we hung up, and I quickly entered a deep meditative state as I worked for her. Forty minutes later, I called Martha back as I always do at the end of a telephone session. Her words tumbled out in a rush. She had burst into tears right after we hung up. She realized that she did not have to suffer for George. She actually never needed to suffer for George. Her sense of relief was tangible. Her new insight lifted her spirit. The biggest surprise in this situation was how compassion, rather than guilt, flooded her reality. Compassion arose for herself first and then for her dear George.

Guilt is insidious. For Martha, what seemed like self-less sacrifice for the soul of her departed husband was actually a pervasive guilt that she had let him down and that he was lost in some hellish afterlife. She believed it was up to her to correct the situation. Punishing herself by taking on suffering specifically to obtain his entry ticket to heaven rested on her underlying guilt. When we talked at length about the situation, along with her clarity about having had enough of the pain she brought upon herself, her true compassion began to overtake the guilt. She could then express her love and concern for George in a different way. She could also trust the profound compassion of God for George's soul.

TUNE IN TO RESONANCE

Reflect on the situations in your life where you may have invited suffering because you felt guilt about something. Imagine the grace of forgiveness coming to you like a fine rain. As you let the mist settle around you and you feel its soothing touch, ask it to dissolve any attachment you may have to acting out of guilt. Let it wash away this counterfeit form of compassion.

Can we actually ask for suffering and does God or the Universe specifically assign suffering to us? Are we

A PERSONAL

PRACTICE

FOR YOU

A PERSONAL PRACTICE
OF RESONANCE

Allow these pictures to create a sacred space for you to explore the nine gateways of practice. As your awareness shifts into the mystery, you can use the accompanying text to engage your mind. With practice your mind will become quiet and expansive. May each gateway give you a blessing of healing and renewal.

Appreciation and Awareness

I allow my awareness to expand

My view widens further and further

As each increment of awareness opens, I notice the changes

Today I appreciate my level of freedom

I see beyond the outer shell of those who challenge me

I see and appreciate the diamond inner core of each being—the God-self that resides undiminished in each of us

I embrace that core self within me

Intuition and Action

I trust my inner self

I can reach that place in me that is connected to all that is

I recognize the nudges toward optimal action that come through the all that is

If I make a mistake, I will notice what prompted the action that was not accurate

I will not harshly judge myself

I return to an easy and relaxed confidence

I act in alignment with my intuition

Presence and Communication

I find silence within

I maintain deep peace within

I invite communication with universal presence

I receive that communication with all my senses

I rely on inner knowing

I call forth my wisdom self

Connection and Protection

I look to connection with the One for my safety

I am not distracted by limited expressions of protection

I allow the ringing temple bell, the prayer, the sacred symbols to point the way

I explore the growth of my conscious connection with universal Oneness

I relax without need to grasp any false safety

I look to truth that guides me

I trust my connection and rest within universal protection

Balance and Harmony

I embrace the quality of balance for my body

What is out of balance transforms

I send the quality of harmony to all the cells of my body

I embrace the quality of balance for my mind

What is out of balance transforms

I send the quality of harmony to all my thoughts and actions

I embrace the quality of balance for my spirit

What is out of balance transforms

I send the quality of harmony to all my lifetimes and my soul

I embrace the quality of balance for my community

What is out of balance is blessed with transformation

I send the quality of harmony to all my relations

COMPASSION AND CLARITY

I treasure my moments of clarity

I treasure the experience of compassion

I see where clarity leads me

In deep meditation I pause, wait peacefully

Compassion arises

Attention and Focus

I listen to the wonder of simple miracles

I flow with the constancy of renewal

I appreciate all these miracles of my biology and . . .

I pay attention to the deep silence of creation's pulse

And I naturally flow into focus

As I focus, I trust the outcome

I return to quiet attention when focus fades

I flow as naturally as the tides move in response to moon, gravity, landscape, and mystery

SENSITIVITY AND JOY

I greet and welcome all aspects of my true self

I know my nature ever more deeply

I honor the sensitive design within me

I allow that design to inform me at all levels

I pay attention to my insights

I realize that I can wake joyfully

Move joyfully

Work joyfully

I realize that I can sleep in peace

Resonance and Transformation

I seek my unique resonance

I listen to be in tune

I embrace well-being that comes through resonance

The deep current of transformation continually moves me

I notice when I respond from joy

I let go and trust

I do not cling to anything

I am moved to a deeper resonance with all that is

Union . . . Oneness . . . ever flowing

I walk the path of the Mystery
My heart overflows with gratitude

"taught" through states of disease and loss? As a species, we have struggled with these questions for millennia. Our ideas about the reasons for suffering range from original sin that nips at our heels and catches us when we least expect, to the results of karma of our own accumulated actions in this or another life. We have concluded that it is either our direct fault or the fault of some basic nature of humankind.

Theologians have a technical name for this topic—theodicy. Thomas Aquinas said, "God allows evil to happen in order to bring a greater good therefrom." One logic based argument proceeds as follows: "If God is perfectly good, He must want to abolish evil; if He is unlimitedly powerful, He must be able to abolish all evil; but evil exists; therefore either God is not perfectly good or He is not unlimitedly powerful."[2] In more ancient times, particularly in Egypt, the presence of many gods at war for control of the universe explained struggle and suffering. In the Buddhist tradition, suffering is addressed as a condition of the world of illusion, which does not include God and therefore cannot blame God.

Philosophical ideas range from there is no God to the necessity of free will in which we choose evil and create our own suffering. That affliction brings important lessons and gives meaning to misery is an idea afloat in our culture. I've repeatedly heard from clients who suffered through a debilitating disease and equally debilitating treatment that during the process they learned so much. They would not ask for such suffering, but are grateful for gifts of insight and experiences of care they received during their illness. Does that justify the pain? Questions hang in the air without answers that truly satisfy.

I have no logical answers for myself on these issues. The polarities of thought that either God is impotent, evil, or does not exist do not satisfy me. My own experience of being conscious in some other dimension beyond my physical body changed my personal way of framing the issue of theodicy. I was in a place where there was no suffering, no longing for anything, and no desire to change anything. Perfect peace, joy, and the union of belonging was profound. And yet after returning from that "place" I wrote, "I choose to return to the dense confines of flesh and blood, to the measured pace of earth."

The separateness and tough pain of earthly existence is a mystery. I do not understand it and have found no logical thought process that can make sense of it. I leave it as an unsolved mystery and continue to alleviate as much suffering as possible for myself and others.

How Does Compassion Move Us?

Significantly more than an emotion of care or concern, compassion is a state of being. In that regard compassion is not a static quality; it leads to action. Intriguing new studies show that the normal human brain is functionally and structurally organized to sense distress in others. So even the image of someone suffering causes specific neurons in the prefrontal lobe of our brain to fire up, a location that is known to be associated with the impulse to leap to assist. If we want the leap to be effective then clarity is an essential companion along the way. In that sense, compassion is not a generalized phenomenon; it is specific to each situation, and it is especially engaged when our minds and hearts are most clear. Quite different in tone from pity, which often leads to stagnation and a long-lasting state of emotional sadness, compassion looks for an outlet in the form of helping deeds.

Compassion can be expressed in words, facial expression, body language, and total silence. When we visit a friend or family member in the hospital, oftentimes we feel compelled to talk for the sake of talking. The content may be about last night's baseball game, a favorite television show, or a litany of how well everything is going for the patient. "You'll be fine. Just a few more days, and you'll be good as new."

A weary look on the face of the bedridden patient says it all. The banter is tiring and not necessarily true. Here is a place and time for clarity to inform compassionate action to be quiet, fully present, and relate to the patient with a simple touch on the shoulder or hand. The need to chatter emerges from the visitor's discomfort with the hospital setting, the illness of the loved one, or simply an inability to find the right thing to say. There may be no "right" thing to say. To be a comforting presence who can relax in a connected silence is the expression of compassion that brings comfort to the ailing person.

There are situations that challenge our compassion particularly when misunderstanding comes up. On my first trip to Bali when I worked with Jero Tapakan, I became embroiled in one of those circumstances. At Jero Tapakan's kind invitation, I was a guest in her family compound. I had been there for four days and simply needed more exercise than the short walk from where we ate to the sitting porch to my room. I was used to at least a two-mile walk every day back home with my dog. There was nothing in particular going on that day in the outskirts of Bangli, and I walked out of the family compound and down the deserted road along acres of brilliantly green rice fields. There were no vehicles, no people, and no critters except the ducks swimming on a few rice fields that had been harvested and subsequently flooded. Those ducks were fun to watch as they tipped upside down to nibble the rice grains that had escaped the huge woven baskets during harvest. While they ate the rice, they fertilized the rice field for the next crop. Their ultimate destination would be dinner for a villager after they were plump and juicy from abundant meals in rice fields.

The day was warm and breezy. The solitude was delicious. The exercise was sorely needed. I returned after 45 minutes to such hubbub. It seemed centered around me, but I did not have a clue what was the matter. Fortunately, that afternoon was the time my translator, Budi, was to visit and enable communication between my hosts and me. He walked into chaos that day. The upshot of it all was that my hosts thought that I was extremely unhappy about something and left to never return. They were worried about me out there on the road by myself. No one among them would ever think to take off on a walk alone, or actually go for a walk at all. There was plenty of exercise in the work they did each day. It was just plain strange for anyone to go for a walk without some specific duty or event. Once we worked out the ups and downs of my being very happy and appreciative of their kindness and hospitality and the quirks of Western ways, all was well. For the next four days of my stay with the family, each time I got up from a table or a bench or appeared outside my room, someone would smile at me and say: "Jalan jalan?" The word *jalan* means "road." Said twice, it meant: "Did I want to go for a walk?" Whoever asked was ready and able to saunter down the road with me. The family was compassionate to me, and some clarity about our cultural differences made for a return to peace and under-standing. In general, clarity can allow us to step back from situations, breathe a little, and proceed with reasonable direction; neither damning nor condoning, but resonating with true compassion.

When a group experiences clarity and compassion the reverberation touches many lives. Friend and colleague Jack Elias recently shared this story from one of his hypnotherapy classes.

> A while back, one of my hypnotherapy students became extremely angry at her fellow students for their lack of punctuality in coming to class. When she couldn't take it another minute, she began voicing her frustration with them, defending her position with the ideas of right and wrong, rude and polite, considerate and inconsiderate, and so on. Everyone in class became annoyed with her for making a mountain out of a molehill. Because it's an experiential class, I asked her to focus on her anger and look into it, to see if the anger might have a deeper cause than being offended by others' rudeness. With a little help, she soon remembered being a little girl in Germany during World War II. She had been visiting her grandparents in the country and had missed the train home. Back in the city, much later than usual, she arrived to find that her home had been destroyed by Allied bombs and her parents killed. If only she had been on time! Maybe she could have had those last precious moments with her parents. She broke into sobs. When her classmates heard this story and witnessed her grief, their irritation with her dissolved. And because she had discovered the real reason for her distress—the real answer to the real quest—she was released from her desperate obsession with being on time.

Everyone in the class now changed their attitude about being on time. Punctuality stopped being a rule to be enforced by some and selfishly ignored or rebelled against by others. Classmates stopped seeing each other as right or wrong, or good or bad, depending upon their choice to be on time or to be late to class. Because choosing to make the effort to be punctual was no longer a point of contention, it became an opportunity to support each other with compassion.

Each person in the group had their own relationship to time and to punctuality, therefore, the changes in each person were somewhat different. How the group consciousness shifted is an inspiring glimpse at how communities may change in ways to live with each other in a more positive and supportive manner. However, there are limitations on the degree of change some individuals can make. For some biology rather than choice seems to play a major role. A prime example of this is a person diagnosed to be a psychopath. The neural construct in the brain of a psychopath is different. A large area of the brain is underdeveloped. The neurons in this region do not grow normally, nor do they make the connections that allow most people to feel empathy for others. Because of this different brain structure, traditional psychotherapy is ineffective in altering their behavior.[3] For them, choosing to change is not an option. But in the future the burgeoning field of neuroplasticity may bring hope to those who suffer from this form of illness.

How Do You Know When You Are Clear?

A reader of my book *Cell-Level Healing* was ardently engaged in the exercises for identifying and clearing blockages. She felt that she had started with many blockages and that they were indeed damaging to her life. Her dedication to the practice was admirable, and she was aware of positive changes that had not happened with other healing modalities. She wondered, *How do I know when I am completely clear?*

This is such an apt question, as most of us live with a familiar and somewhat comfortable degree of muddle and confusion in our everyday lives. What is the experience of clarity? How long does it last? To what degree can I expect relief of blockages?

There is no intellectual checklist that will give us a measure of our percent of clarity. It would be handy to know that I am 85 percent clear and therefore need precisely 27 hours of meditation to achieve full clarity. Such precision is not something we can achieve. Our degree of clarity is partially informed by feedback from friends and associates and from our personal sense—our own perception of how clear we feel. Perhaps we are more aware when we are blocked and feel overwhelmed, confused, crabby, ungrounded, and dissatisfied with life.

Over the course of history human beings have created theoretical models to explain how things work in the world. Over time our perceptions are in fact guided by and informed by these models. After Galileo's model of the heavens was widely accepted we were less likely to think of our home planet as the center of the universe, though many of us can't seem to stop thinking of ourselves as key to all that goes on here. In many ways our reality is based on and shaped by the model we most frequently entertain. At some point we forget that we are using a model at all and instead think we are directly describing reality. The apples continue to fall, therefore Newton's law is reality. Then along comes quantum physics and our understanding is turned upside down. Now our best theorists are searching for a new model, a "theory of everything" to reconcile all of it. Stephen Hawking and an associate have recently weighed in on quantum mechanics, neurobiology, and Newtonian physics by pointing out that we benefit by remembering that our "reality" is in fact model-dependent.[4]

Not only relevant to the physical world of our universe, model-dependent reality is consummately useful in understanding human perception and how we relate to ourselves and our communities. In *The Grand Design,* Stephen Hawking says, "The brain is so good at model building that if people are fitted with glasses that turn the images in their eyes upside down, their brains, after a time, change the model so that they again see things the right way up."[5] He also suggests that there may not be one theory that fits the entire scope of reality. Moreover, he asserts that multiple theories are applicable and convenient to use and reflect reality just fine, and this might just be the way of the universe. Our pursuit of one unifying theory is not resonant with the reality of different perceivers. To acknowledge and celebrate our perceiver/observer role in reality making along with accepting many models that describe different aspects of the multidimensional universe makes so much sense. We can also be wary of accepting any one model as reality itself. Just as the word is not the thing, but rather a symbol representing the thing, a model is useful only up to a certain point. That is why we can neither apply the Newtonian model to the nanosphere nor the quantum model to building bridges.

We can apply this to the question of how to know when we are clear. Possibly we never fully know when we are clear, and the goal is not to achieve some standard-ized 100 percent clarity. Most likely, our experience of clarity is multidimensional. To be resonant at any point in time and place with ourselves and with our envi-ronment speaks of clarity. Disharmony is a sure signal that clarity is compromised. And, if we are clear at one moment, the next may bring a situation in which the model changes and we lose clarity. The two qualities of this chapter dance with each other. Compassion helps maintain a state of clarity, and clarity informs the abid-ing presence of compassion.

THE PRACTICE: COMPASSION AND CLARITY

We have all experienced moments of clarity and felt the impulse for compassionate action. How can we deepen our clarity and fine-tune our natural impulse to serve?

As you settle into a quiet space for your practice, slowly bring your mind's focus to the center of your chest. We'll call that the heart space. What is there?

Allow what comes in response to the question to dissolve by sending light to the thought or simply relaxing with the thought as it dissipates. Go deeper in your settling to as expansive and quiet a place in your heart space as you can. As you look, there will eventually be nothing to see, and you can rest beyond the models, refer-ence points, and concepts that your mind creates. The compassionate pulse of the universe dwells here. Rest in that place as long as is comfortable and practical.

When you naturally shift from that altered state of awareness, be open to unbidden clarity. The best such moments are when clear ideas seem to spontaneously float into your awareness or when they seem to pop into mind without struggle.

Your practice enables you to be a receiver of spiritual insight that is resonant with compassion and clarity. You can return again and again, more quickly each time, to this expansively resonant inner temple deep in your own heart space.

As familiar and comfortable as a true home, this practice is a place to live.

CHAPTER 7

ATTENTION AND
FOCUS

What is deep listening? . . .
Give more of your life to this listening . . .
I should sell my tongue and buy a thousand ears . . .

— RUMI

A laser pumped intense red light at a frequency of 694 nanometers from an industrial ruby. The beam of light was aimed directly into a circular glass container full of an opaque dye. As the ruby laser hummed away, the dye sat, looking impenetrably cloudy. In another instant it flashed clear as the purest water, and in yet another instant, it flashed back to thickly white and opaque. The flash lasted just five nanoseconds, an incomprehensibly short burst. The properties of the ultrashort pulse of light were strange indeed. It was hard science. We were in an advanced laser technology laboratory—but it looked like something out of *Star Trek*.

Using the extraordinary properties of the Q-switched laser, we were studying the pigments in fish skin cells. The clear nature of the surface of these cells made the project possible. The basic science of this work elucidated the vulnerability of the pigment, melanin, to intense ruby light; and the applied aspect of the work enabled salmon to be branded when they were fingerlings—before they swam from fresh water to the ocean. This allowed us to track the timing and location of salmon migration from their place of hatching to the ocean and back from the ocean to breed and lay eggs in fresh water streams. Crucial to the preservation of salmon as a species and as a fishing industry, this information is used by agencies such as National Marine Fisheries to regulate when and where salmon can be caught.

Melanin in fish has the same molecular structure as in humans; and wherever it is found in nature, it's one of the most resistant molecules known. It can be boiled it in sulfuric acid for days without disrupting its structural integrity, but we found that we could vaporize this tough protein with one pulse of red light.

To work directly with fish melanin took weeks of preparation. When all adjustments were completed, the high-power laser jolted the dye-filled cell that served as a shutter mechanism, a nanosecond pulse of light was unleashed, and the mirrors did their job directing the light to a metal target where atoms were stripped of their electrons. Right before our eyes an olive-sized ball of light danced in the middle of the room. The plasma sizzled and sparkled. We felt like mad scientists as we gaped at the miniature sun we had created.

Now it was time to change our focus. Once again we aimed the ruby light through the unique shutter arrangement of the dye cell, and the nanosecond burst of light jetted around the room and arrived at our research target: a water-filled chamber that contained a living Chinook salmon fry (small fish—about six inches long). The humans in the lab were all careful to keep their fingers well out of the path of the laser light as keratin in human skin absorbs this type of laser light, and the pulse was powerful enough to badly burn an unwary finger.

When the pulse reached the fish skin, the response was spectacularly unremarkable. The fish did not even twitch. Weeks later a round black spot about a half inch across was distinctly visible on the fish's side. Was it a burn? No. Our studies with the electron microscope showed no damage whatsoever to the transparent skin or scales of the fish. However, the pigment granules within the specialized pigment cells had been completely vaporized by the laser pulse.[1]

We had anticipated that the skin would not be damaged and that the effect would focus on pigment, but seeing it happen was still astonishing. The pigment granules vaporized inside the pigment cells without damage to the surrounding cellular structures or to adjacent tissues. No laser light passed beyond to damage any other part of the fish. Today these very same lasers are used to remove tattoos. Unfortunately for humans our skin, unlike fish skin, does absorb ruby-laser light, so the treatment can be painful.

I look back on that research with appreciation for the power of focus, a focus so refined that it could touch individual pigment granules and leave all else unharmed. And I cannot help but compare the laser's power to instantaneously clarify the dark pigment to the times when inspiration flashes forth in the mind at the moment we are open.

I've found the quality of focus in healing work to be akin to the laser in power and refinement. Rapt attention allows the focus to be guided to the key location. These two qualities, the subjects of this chapter, establish a kind of attention that overrides mind chatter and preconceived ideas. We can listen to our innate wisdom and to our subtle senses to enhance our perception. We listen with both inner and outer knowing. Questions to these several levels of guidance and to our own body can promote active listening. What does the body call for? What does one group of cells need from other parts of the body? How does the model of a healthy body show us the way to consciously promote health and an optimally functioning community of cells within us?

Here lies the heart of the effectiveness of cell-level resonance. To develop the skill of attention and the proficiency to focus clears the way to seek the most effective treatments for healing. This works for our own healing, and it works when we are assisting others. Peg's story illustrates how this happens.

Peg called me for an appointment. She lived on the East Coast and wondered if the expanse of country from Massachusetts to Washington State would compromise the ability for her to benefit from a session. My experience has been that the distance does not matter one bit. Clients in England, Australia, South America, and Mexico have had equally strong healing results as those who have walked into my office. It appears that this work is not limited by distance and not dependent on proximity.

Peg had a serious case of plantar fasciitis in her left foot that had plagued her for over a year. Her hiking and walking outings were curtailed to nearly nothing, which shut down her main source of exercise and a cherished activity that supported her sense of well-being. Ordinary walking in daily life was fraught with pain at every step.

Our phone session in the spring was an uncertain exploration for Peg—an outreach that was purely an experiment mixed with equal amounts of desperation and hope. After our initial conversation that March during which I heard the history of her particular problems, we hung up our phones. Peg lay down on her bed in the privacy of her home in Cambridge, Massachusetts, and I sat in my treatment room in Seattle attuned to guidance for the best way to help her. I followed that guidance and focused healing energy to Peg.

At the end of the session—about ten minutes before the top of the hour, I called her back. Immediately she said, "I didn't feel anything." I assured her that I would be sending healing in my morning meditations for the next five days to support the work we had begun. I also advised her to hold off for several days on making an assessment as to whether the session was helpful to her, since most people feel the benefits some days after our work. I did not hear back from Peg for four months when she called for another appointment. "I must tell you what happened after my first healing time with you," she said. She explained that not only during the session, but throughout that entire day and evening, nothing had changed. Her foot hurt as much as it had the entire year. However, the next day the pain on the bottom of her foot went away only to be replaced by terrible and strange sensations on the top of her foot. Within another day's time, however, the top of her foot returned to normal—pain-free. For the last four months between sessions, Peg had enjoyed trouble-free hiking and walking. I could hear her smile as she expressed a heightened appreciation for the simple ability to walk that its loss had brought into focus.

How did the healing session work from my end as a practitioner? First, I listened to Peg with the usual sense of hearing her voice tell me about her situation. A deeper level of hearing happens in the first few minutes of any session. The listening seems to reach throughout my body, and I feel the issue at hand. I am also asking for guidance and relax to listen for nudges that come as either kinesthetic or subtle knowing. In that relaxed state I find that the guidance is accurate and reliable. We can do this for ourselves too. Let's explore how to develop the skill of listening effectively.

Is There a Healing Protocol to Follow?

From my perspective as a healing facilitator, there is no step-by-step protocol; although, there are some guidelines. In my first book, *Cell-Level Healing,* I explored how to identify blockages, clear those blockages, and support flow in the body. These three practices are the basis of any healing work I do. Each person is different, of course. That also means that each approach is somewhat different. Listening and sensing the unique needs of individuals allow the work to be precise, effective, and long lasting. In Peg's situation, it was important to establish a flow of energy throughout her body, not solely in her foot. She had related some troubling issues with family members that were in the past but continued to be upsetting. Although we did not talk at length about those issues, I did address them in the energy work phase of the session with the intention to soften their impact. Had those issues been current or more bothersome to her, I would have referred her to a therapist to assist her with the cognitive and behavioral aspects of such traumas.

For Peg the foot problem was not directly related to the previous emotional challenges, therefore, the clearing proceeded rapidly and the center of attention shifted naturally to the physical dimension. At that point my work addressed the inflammation in her foot. My primary learning mode is visual, and my work as a scientist included hundreds of hours of image assessment with the electron microscope. It is no wonder that image is a strong part of my practice as well. Images just seem to come to me. In Peg's case, I actively saw the cells and subcellular processes that could remove inflammation. Each of us as healing facilitators may use a variety of techniques as we expand our search for the most natural and effective approach for our own healing and for assisting others.

I must admit that I do not know precisely what worked so well for Peg. On the other hand, I do know that listening to guidance and following that path to focus healing energy uniquely for her felt clear, right, and overwhelmingly peaceful for me as the facilitator. I also trust those sensations and feelings as I continue working for each client in meditation during the five mornings after a formal session.

Would Peg's foot have healed spontaneously on its own? It's certainly possible. However, we are both plainly grateful that she is better and out in the greater world enjoying the freedom of movement with two comfortable feet. The exact mechanism of healing is unknown at this point. The observation of unusual healing effects after energy work and prayer, however, builds a body of data that informs us of the potential for healing outside of our ordinary understanding. When someone experiences 365 days of severe foot pain, an hour's session for healing, and two days later, complete relief from pain, it is a cause for celebration. The experience is unforgettable.

Cause and Effect in Healing

The role of cause and effect in personal health touches us all sooner or later. Is my diagnosis a punishment? Is it a lesson long rejected or missed? The theme of illness as a penalty for a known or unknown transgression is deeply embedded in our cultural roots and psyches. But such notions may, in fact, keep us from the resources of healing that are all around us and within us. If we listen only to the plaintive voice of blame and judgment, the voice of healing and hope fades to a whisper.

Clearly we know some causes of disease. We are exposed to bacteria and viruses repeatedly, and fall ill from time to time. Our immune system is highly tuned to recognize invading organisms and continues to "learn" as we age. We are equipped with inner tools of biology to fight off infections and keep us alive and well. When this system fails in the sense that we become ill, our tendency is to ask why. There are times when a clear answer is there. We had been stressed at work, unhappy at home, running on little sleep, or hanging out with kindergarteners who all had colds. The immune system was compromised by the stressors and overwhelming exposure to cold or flu viruses. It is clear that stress degrades the strength of the immune system, and taking steps to destress our lives is appropriate and useful. With diseases more complex than the flu, we often don't have a clear sense of cause, nor do our doctors. I've found at such times that the best approach is to let go of "cause" and face up to "what is." In this way, we can concentrate all of our energies on returning to health.

Major healing crises, although not welcome, do come into our lives. Diane called me from Connecticut. She was newly diagnosed with an aggressive form of breast cancer. She was convinced that her prayer to expand her prominence as a woman of wisdom had actually brought on the cancer. She was sure that the answer to her request was a God-given affliction of a forceful disease. Diane was so certain that she quickly began to accept the cancer as a means to greatness. Someone else might see the illness as punishment for the request. I spoke with her at some length about how to uncouple this cause and effect idea from the cancer, and how to allow her expansion into a new vision for her work to continue independent of the diagnosis. We talked about how to shift her focus to enable all the methods of treatment to support her return to robust health. This very smart and savvy woman got the distinction right away. The lift in her voice said it all— she was already engaged in a new approach that could carry her through treatment and simultaneously support her desire for a larger footprint of service.

Each of us can ask for insight for what may need to change in us that we may be more fully whole and joyful. Though sometimes the need for personal change, be it physical or behavioral, presents itself at the most unexpected times.

I had a whopping good lesson of this recently at a well-known retreat center. A respected yoga teacher was conducting a workshop near my cabin. I walked by his class window on my way to my place. I was surprised to see him leap toward me from the other side of the window, waving his arms in a threatening gesture with a ferocious look on his face. He seemed furious that someone would dare to walk by his personal sanctuary yet his behavior was likely more disturbing to his class. I wanted to ask him to remember his yoga. Since there was no opportunity to speak with him privately to work this out, I had to look inside myself and realize that there are times when the work is fully our own. What I did with this situation was to remember my yoga and to look at the causes within me or around me that push my own aggressive tendencies into expression. Such outbursts are hard on our bodies. When equanimity wanes, our blood pressure rises, our digestion is tweaked, our neurons cease replication, and our immune system is impeded in its vital work. The physical damage is mine and mine alone. Pull the plug on anger and associated stress, and neurons divide—repopulate our brain—and the other body functions return to a cheerful if not blissful hum. Ironically, this is the goal of yoga itself, to return the mind-body complex to union, wholeness, and peace. The outcome for me of the situation was a rollicking good belly laugh at myself along with a decision to avoid the classroom window and thereby tempt neither the grouchy yoga teacher nor myself. I cannot change him or his behavior but I can certainly change mine.

TUNE IN TO RESONANCE

As you relax into a deep part of yourself, breathe to your core—to the deepest sense of self you can reach. If you believe that your thoughts alone have created a difficult condition in your life, allow that attachment to dissolve. Experiment with letting the mystery of the complexity of cause and effect be simply that—a mystery. You may never fully know the causative conditions for your situation. Can you let go of the desire to have a definitive explanation? Now imagine that you can gather all your energy and direct that flow toward healing, well-being, and a new awareness of the fullness of physical health.

Attention Beyond Methodology

There is an abundance of material available these days for learning methods of healing. We can study medicine, nursing, acupuncture, psychiatry, psychotherapy, chakra balancing, EFT (Emotional Freedom Technique), meridian flow or at least 75 branded, titled, and trademarked methods of energy healing. Training is an essential starting place in most fields of human endeavor. I remember how I felt when I finished my doctorate in biophysics. I was ready to pursue research as a trained and credentialed professional. Yes, I knew how to operate electron microscopes, how to interpret data from micrographs, and how to write and speak about the research with others. I thought I was fully trained, fully capable of conducting dazzling research. I was off to a National Institutes of Health–funded research center for my postdoctoral fellowship, but it did not take long to realize that my education, rich and valuable as it was, could not serve as a template for success in every research project. I had so much to learn and so much to experience. That was the beginning of my lifelong enchantment with learning.

To be alert and attentive was one of the early requirements that allowed me to evolve from a newly hatched fledgling, find my wings, and explore the joys of flying as a research scientist. Each project had its own requirements and its own path of progress to useful information and finally to publication. Just as each client has her or his own constellation of life experiences, bodily sensations, beliefs, and needs.

In each profession, training has an important place. Experience builds on the educational foundation, but with surprises at every turn. How many times did I exclaim, "They never told me about this! I don't know how to handle this—it wasn't covered in any text or lecture." Creativity rather than rote memorization, adaptability rather than rigidity, listening rather than wooden-headed plodding is essential for success.

To learn how to deeply pay attention requires that we go beyond techniques. Please hear that I do not think there is anything wrong with training, mentors, or schools of healing for self or others. To repeat protocols perfectly is not the essence, however, of expertise in any endeavor—especially not in healing work. For example, no two people with arthritis are exactly the same, have the same etiology or expression of symptoms, and do not respond to medication in exactly the same way. When someone enters my treatment room for a healing session, I must be wholly present, fully in listen mode, and not presume that because I've worked with someone else with the same diagnosis, that I can apply exactly the same strategy for the new client. The same applies to subsequent visits with the same client. Each time is unique to itself, and each person has changed in the intervening time. To be alert at every moment is the heart of listening and the key to cell-level work.

TUNE IN TO RESONANCE

What if this moment was the only moment in time? How would you listen? Could you relax with keen

awareness of the precious breath you now inhale? Could
you allow a blessing of the fullness of grace to touch you
with exquisite kindness in this one moment?

There are many levels of listening. In the woods,
when trees are laden with snow, a crackling sound por-
tends a branch on its way to the ground. If the crackle
is directly above your head, musing about your quarterly
taxes may prevent the kind of listening that propels you
out of harm's way. A clear mind and the appropriate focus
include an assessment of where the branch about to fall is
located and that informs the winter hiker of the appropriate response. Run, *now!*

Full of sounds that we heed, our environment is one
of the first and most important places we listen and learn
to interpret. Equally important, the skill of hearing our
own body can be developed and refined. A scraped knee
or a cut that bleeds gets attention. What about the more
subtle symptoms in our body? Do we notice when those
need to be heeded? Without creating a frantic and overly
attentive style, deep listening to the body can be one of
our most valuable assets in early detection of changes that
we, our physicians, and healers can work with. We develop
listening skills as we train to recognize the more and more
subtle messages that we've previously missed or chosen
not to see.

Our own limitations may seem like the bars of a prison.
When the world and everyone in it appears unfriendly
and menacing, how can we shift our focus, dissolving
the bars of captivity? How can we tune into a higher perspective? In the laser laboratory the shimmering plasma
in the middle of the room came to life when the cloudy
dye flashed clear, shining light into the room. When we
open ourselves to the pure energy of our true self, from

the universe that lives inside of us, how does that light change how we see the world? How does a clear pulse of giving, rather than grasping, heal a discouraged moment? The world has not changed, but we now see the luminous beauty of creation and our place in it.

Essentials of Focus

How does focus feel?

We know the kind of focus that strains the eyes, neck, and emotions. There is another way—one that is observant, yet relaxed. The first step to apply deep listening for healing is to develop a practice of focus with the latter attributes. All the groundwork of full attention creates a trustworthy platform on which to embark upon the best kinds of focus.

Perhaps there are fewer distractions in places like Bali, and that, combined with the skillful ability of my teacher, Jero Mangku Srikandi, taught me how to maintain a steady and prolonged state of focus. That kind of mindfulness supported my ability to meditate, to enjoy the moment, to experience an abiding calm, and to maintain a healing state at the cellular level. The lessons were intense and came about through tests for which I had no instruction and no forewarning as to what would happen or be expected of me. One of her inimitable tests was set on the sacred grounds of a small temple on Mount Agung. I could look up to the clouds that hovered near the 11,000-foot summit and out to an expansive view of rice fields, terrace after terrace, and the ocean which seemed to go on forever.

The entryway to the temple had an unusually large open space. I was familiar with the necessity of an initial ceremony when we entered a temple. In all the dozen other temples where Jero had taken me, she had me either sit just inside the entrance or stand while she chanted and sought permission from the guardian spirits of the place for us to enter and proceed with ceremonies. This time was different. We arrived late in the afternoon with a retinue of people who brought food and sleeping pads and a blanket for each person. We settled down to sleep after a simple dinner of rice with a mixture of green stuff, most likely vegetables. I never asked what was actually in the food I was offered, just ate with gratitude and appetite.

The morning was beautiful—swathed in mist and rolling clouds that revealed and obscured the view by turns. I'd learned to trust the timing and flow of temple visits and the requisite test I was to undergo. Although I had been through a dozen such events, each in a different location, I still marveled that I'd ever passed a single test. This time I had been instructed to dress in a new and specifically patterned sarong, a lacy top that women wear in ceremony, and the required temple scarf, which was tied around my waist. I entered the wide-open space directly inside the temple entrance. Jero emerged from a side entrance adorned in a manner I'd not seen in the previous nine years of working with her. Her hair hung down—the first I'd seen it other than in a bun on the back of her head. Not only was it unfettered, it was long. Her hair swished against the backs of her knees. Jero's blouse was red, as was her sarong, and her feet were bare. She danced the distance from a hidden entrance at the side of the temple to the middle of the space where I was waiting. My translator then, and only then, informed me that I was to catch Jero's forearm and grasp it with my hand. How agile and swift this 60-plus Balinese woman showed herself to be as she dipped and spun, swirled and dashed about the open temple yard. I thought it would be easy to move right up to her and grab her arm. Not so! When I did get close enough to reach out toward her, she darted away, obviously enjoying the game. I was baffled. I could not catch her.

Something deeply internal stirred in me, and I felt myself settle into calmness not unlike an altered state that I enter during meditation. Time seemed to shift, seemed to expand, so that a clock second felt like several minutes. Again, as in meditation, all sensory input dropped away except the singular focal point which now was Jero's arm. A profound sense of peace welled up from somewhere deep inside of me. I was no longer driven to perform but very simply stepped toward her with calm focus, reached out, gently touched her arm, and took hold of it with my hand. The dance, the ceremony, and the test were over. I passed. The situation had shifted from baffled frustration to the success of merely grasping her arm the instant that I stopped struggling, and achieved proper focus. Time seemed to stretch out as I did that. My perception of Jero's movements changed from swift to long and slow. The reach that had been so impossibly difficult became easy.

TUNE IN TO RESONANCE

Imagine yourself with your own teacher (that may be an inner teacher or an actual person in any field of endeavor). She or he has asked you to do something extraordinary, and you are baffled at how to respond, let alone how to perform the requested task. Notice your own tendencies. Are you afraid? Are you calculating five strategies with a plus and minus list for each one? Are you about ready to run away?

Release all self-judgment. Relax, relax, relax. Listen for the nudge inside of yourself that will move you to respond in the most appropriate and efficacious way.

Is there something in your life that you are pursuing? Apply this pattern as you visualize success in your pursuit: relax, focus, listen, move toward your goal. Celebrate! We can apply this to something as ordinary as getting to work on time. Traffic is snarled. Time is passing. What to do? Sit back in the car seat, relax, calmly focus on arriving at work. Place your attention on your inner knowing, and allow a sense of guidance to shift the challenge and the perception of time. You may surprise yourself and be at work on time, or not quite make the clock but arrive with calm good humor.

The idea of focus as a good and useful practice had moved for me from theory to an indelible knowing. Practicing focus has stayed with me now for a decade and is central to healing work for myself, and in my formal work as a healing facilitator. In addition, focus during healing work enhances one's ability to receive healing energy.

Each of us can train our mind to focus in meditation, and in being calmly and fully present in our encounters within our self, and in our encounters with others. The skill that develops can be demonstrated with EEG testing, as I discovered about five years after I had completed my training with Jero. I was at Nihon University in Tokyo, Japan. With 125 wet sensors attached to my skull, the EEG data showed that I had an atypical and remarkable ability to focus. Dr. Akio Mori, a neuroscience specialist at the university, said that he had not seen anyone with my level of focus in his 40 years of testing brain function in individuals. I am grateful to Jero for opening my awareness to the possibility of training my mind. As I think back to the laser laboratory and the dye-filled cell that could absorb light only so long before it became a clear lens, I see a parallel in spiritual practice. What does it take for any one of us to become transparent? Jero helped me throw my personal dye-filled cell away, and transmit a steady beam of energy. I know that focus applied to healing enables the work to reach deeply into the cellular arena, where it can be most effective. To hold focus without distraction is the goal of applied listening.

The following practice is offered to help you develop your own skill in combining listening and focus.

THE PRACTICE: ATTENTION AND FOCUS

From a relaxed position, perhaps lying down on a comfortable couch, imagine that you can touch the inside of your consciousness, as if it were a tangible and moveable energy field. In your mind's eye or with your hands, slowly expand that field until you can imagine that you are afloat within an expanded and safe energy sphere.

Take your time and enjoy this expanded state while you pay attention without worry, and without struggling for answers. The important messages come when your mind is worry free and receptive. If you are working with a particular disease or health condition, listen for guidance about how to enhance your medical treatment with meditation or visualization. Then begin to focus your awareness on the specific cells that need your full attention. You can now consciously bring that expanded state close to your body and into the cell population that is in need of healing. In a sense, it is like opening your arms wide to receive healing blessing, and subsequently accepting that energy and drawing it into your body with single-minded awareness free of distraction.

When you find yourself at ease and experienced with the above meditation you may find this second one to also be beneficial. Again, from a relaxed body position, imagine that your consciousness can gently float above your body. What shape is that part of you? Can you shift the shape? Can you move the shape higher, lower, or from side to side? After exploring the parameters of the shape of your consciousness, allow yourself to open up to deep listening.

Beyond guidance, beyond receiving a message, let the listening be for the pulse of the universe, for the hum of your own consciousness. Now imagine that streams of golden light flow to you from a perfectly compassionate and safe source of the universe—however you may name that source. Your floating self can absorb the light and focus it back to your physical body for renewal and healing. When you feel complete in the practice, welcome your floating consciousness to come fully back and merge with your mind and the sacred ground of your body. The 100 trillion cells that serve your body will be thrilled.

CHAPTER 8

SENSITIVITY AND JOY

Wearing the body-robe, I have been busy in the market,
weighing and arguing prices.
Sometimes I have torn the robe off
with my own hands and thrown it away . . .
When someone feels jealous,
I am inside the hurt and the need to possess.
When anyone is sick, I feel feverish and dizzy.
I am cloud and rain being released,
Then the meadow as it soaks in.

— RUMI

Elise was all of three years old, smart, audacious, and beautiful. She was one of those children that people at the shopping mall stop to admire. The world clearly seemed to be her cup of tea, her playground, and her delight.

One night her mother woke to Elise's loud cries. Mom immediately went into Elise's room and was concerned, because this was exceedingly unusual behavior for her self-confident child. "Something is here" the daughter whispered between sobs. "I'm scared."

Mom asked Elise where the something was and what it looked like. Her tiny hand trembled a bit as she pointed toward the clothes closet, its door open as usual. "It's dark and scary and moves around." Then mom said a most curious thing—for a mom. "Together we'll tell the dark thing to leave. It must leave and not come back. We can send it away."

They did just that and Elise was immediately relieved, felt safe again, and curled up in her mother's arms to go back to sleep. At this tender age, she learned several things. There was help close at hand. She was not alone. Her perception was validated and not dismissed. She was supported and learned how to deal with an unfriendly spirit, or hallucination, or whatever such things are in the reality of a child's mind. The exact nature, height, depth, or actuality of such an apparition is unknown, but many children experience similar phenomena. If parents tell them that there is nothing there, quit crying, and to go back to sleep, an opportunity is lost to validate the natural sensitivity we all seem to bring into this world. The child may then be left with fear and uncertainty about their own perception. Elise learned the power of command and that she can call on allies. Her natural joy in life was there in full force in the morning when she woke.

Most of us didn't have such positive, empowering responses to our midnight fears. I've talked with clients who learned to keep their fears locked up deep inside out of a greater fear of punishment or scorn from a parent who dismissed the possibility of "something scary" in the closet. This is unfortunate. As kids in this situation, we either shut down the ability to perceive such phenomena or react with instantaneous terror at any hint of an unseen presence. We stop trusting our perceptions, stop seeing, stop listening to our inner senses. When any nonphysical incident happens, we assume it is something bad. What if an angel visited us? How can we discern what is good and what is not good when our primary teachers—our parents—do not honor the validity of our experiences? As children, we are lucky if we can find a grandparent, auntie, or someone who can guide us if our parents cannot. As adults, we can find resources from our own inner knowing, from experienced teachers, and from books, but our skills may be rusty at first.

Sensitivity has a wide range of meaning. It is defined variously as responsive, receptive, aware, perceptive, insightful, and easily hurt, easily upset, touchy, and vulnerable. A part of the sensitive nature can be expressed as empathetic—compassionate, able to understand another's feelings at such a deep level that there is a blurring of identity. There are ultrasensitive people, moderately sensitive people, and those who seem insensitive. I hear both ends of the spectrum in my work. There are those who emphatically want to stop being as sensitive as they are and those who want to turn up their sensitivity. Spiritual practice has a way of enhancing sensitivity and expanding empathy. Spiritual practice also can give a place of refuge where the ultrasensitive can find solace and protection from overwhelming input.

When I was in the Philippines and working with Roberto Pidal, he asked me to consider doing two retreats with different Catholic nuns as part of my three-month sojourn. I was excited about the idea and had never done a personal retreat before, and here was the opportunity to be embedded with two very different groups of sisters. I had just spent a week cloistered with the deeply silent and meditative Carmelite sisters at their convent outside of Baguio on Luzon, the main island of the Philippines. The second week was with the Sisters of Saint Paul who had quite a different calling—one that was more social and interactive in the community. One morning, after mass, I sat on my bed in deep silence. My eyes were closed. I felt the room shift subtly but could not ascertain exactly what changed. Barely opening my eyes, I squinted into the simple room. At the far corner I saw a tall shimmering white presence. I blinked my eyes, and it did not go away. I asked in that place inside of me where I'd discovered that truth could be discerned, if this was a good presence. There was no question that goodness had entered my room and that I was blessed by an angelic presence. As I relaxed into the joyous feeling, the sense of time disappeared. I do not know how long I sat transfixed by the glowing white presence that remained in exactly the same location across the room. There was a light knock on my door, and the Mother Superior opened my door and popped her head in. I don't remember if I acknowledged her or broke my gaze, but she closed the door right away, and I heard her walk down the hall. In a short time another knock came on my door and a different nun bustled right into my room with an enormous plate of food. There was rice, fruit, cookies—enough to last me for a week. She placed the platter on a table beside my bed and left. By then, the angel had also left. I was sad that the experience was over but grateful for the blessing of what I had seen and felt. As I nibbled on the delicious tropical fruits, I marveled at the blessing I had received. Later I found out that the head nun, quite a substantial woman herself, had worried that the Carmelites had not fed me enough and that I was languishing in my room in a famished state. My fixed gaze and motionless body had caused her concern, and her cure was a sumptuous plate of food.

I was more in awe than I realized at the time. I had seen an angel. I was lifted into a state of pure joy and transfixed. It seemed that time stopped. Was I breathing? Most likely all the normal body functions were perking along just fine, but I had no sense of anything other than the luminous being that blessed me. There was no specific message or directive, but ecstasy abounded. Like the near-death experience, the impact of the visitation was so intense that I could not take it all in at the time. What did it mean? How was I to understand this event? Was it real? I came to understand the combination of reality and the blessing—the fact that people did actually heal and their wonderful feedback about their experience—that informed my healing work. There was guidance for the many decisions that would come up for me in the years ahead. I learned to make choices from a logical and a contemplative discernment approach. When logic and meditation are in sync, the whole being feels resonant and harmonious.

What is the Science of Sensitivity?

Sensitivity is a quality of living organisms from single cell amoebas to complex mammals such as humans. There are numerous ways that the cells within us receive and transmit information that is the root of the ability to respond to our inner and outer worlds. One of the most basic levels of communication among the trillions of cells in your body is directly between cells. How do cells manage to do that? They have several ways, all quite ingenious. Cells produce and package small biochemical messages that are released from the surface of their membrane. These bits of information float in the miniscule fluid spaces between cells or roll into the bloodstream and travel 30 trillion cells away to inform the far neighborhood of an upcoming block party, or more realistically, of an injury that requires immune system cells to come to the aid of the injured. When cells are stressed, a similar communication network springs into action as many cells produce the "fight-or-flight" hormones—biochemical messages that, if maintained for an extended period of time, can exhaust all systems.

The biochemistry of relaxation, calmness, and peace that can be induced by meditation, exercise, and even chocolate produces endorphins that trigger positive effects throughout trillions of sensitive, listening, and responding cells. You think the internet can reach a large community quickly? Ten minutes of calm, compassionate thought reaches trillions within you.

Cells also communicate by touch. This is not at all a casual or accidental touch of one cell bumping into its neighbor. Cells produce ultra-small nanotubes that are extensions of the cell membrane and stretch out to touch an adjacent cell. Inside the tiny tube, equally small packets of molecules carry a message to the next-door cell. This forms a chain of transmitted messages between cells. Of course, our nerve cells conduct crucial messages using this method all the time, but the fact is that all cells can communicate with each other by touch. In our immune system, for example, specialized cells called fibrocytes wrap around other specialized cells (T cells) as a means of communicating what the body needs for protection.

Although we may not directly perceive the messages that our cells receive, at some level we process their information stream. These bits of data are subtle: part of the biology of our sensitivity. Think about the instances when your body seemed to respond to something far greater than your conscious mind.

Our own bodies provide us with microscopic models of principles for healthy interconnectivity of mind, body, and spirit. Interestingly, the pattern of information "jumping" a gap to enable the receipt of information or to create an appropriate response can be seen in the most analytical of all our organs: the brain. When a neuron sends its message to another neuron, the electrons that flow along the neuronal membrane do not jump to the next neuron. The message they carry stops at the end of the nerve cell. At that point the message is translated by the cell into neurotransmitters, small molecules that cross the gap between nerves and physically touch the next neuron in line. That nerve cell then translates the neurotransmitter into the message that travels as an electron flow along that cell's membrane until it reaches the end of the cell and the translation action repeats. For example, when you stub your toe, the nerve cells in your toe send messages to other nerve cells that relay the messages to your brain. Each relay involves translation from electrons to neurotransmitters over and over again. This complex process, which involves a number of nerve cells from the toe to the brain, occurs in milliseconds. Our sensitivity is organically built in. Its basis is in our biology.

The Synergy of Sensory and Knowledge-Based Information

We constantly make conscious decisions about life, love, and lunch. Clearly, many of those choices are based on past learning. How much do we mix the details of knowledge based learning with the subtleties of sensitivity? How often have we ignored that subtlety to later realize that it was accurate and would have worked out better had we honored the information? In the context of a healing practice, we purposefully tap into the resonance of those information sources. We turn our attention inward and attune ourselves to the body's rhythms, sensations, and reactions. When we sense that something is amiss within us, deep self awareness may call us to press ourselves and our health-care professionals to look deeper for an underlying issue or disease. The operative words here are: I just know.

Sometimes, however, the operative words may have been "I really don't want to know," and the healing practice may make it possible for you to open to whatever the truth is that your mind, body, and spirit already know. That truth may be that it's time to complete a relationship or job and move on. It may be that a pattern of behaviors isn't healthy for you. It may be that a symptom or a health concern—a persistent physical or emotional discomfort, for instance—simply needs to be checked out. Whatever you find, your deepening connection with your sensitivity will support you through your next steps in ways you might never have imagined before.

A client who had struggled with serious family and health complications for several years while maintaining a demanding career said she began a healing practice as "a last resort." "It was a way to at least stay sane with everything falling apart around me." Within a week after our session, Cynthia was relieved to report that she felt noticeably calmer and more centered, despite continued crises erupting around her. A short time later she told me, a little surprised, that her thinking process had begun to change. She could feel guidance coming from deep inside, and she had begun to take steps in a direction of change she felt drawn to explore. "Not as an escape or as a solution," Cynthia said, "but because at this deep level it just felt right." She wasn't certain where it all would lead, but with each step the next step became clear, and many formidable obstacles melted away, astonishing her and everyone else involved. At the same time, some stubborn snags arose that stalled her progress. At those times, she said her practice—especially her deepening experience of opening to trust her sensitivity and her guidance—and it helped her accept the snags as invitations to pause and listen more closely for information and inner guidance before taking action. Within a matter of a few months, an unexpected job opportunity opened up across the country. Because Cynthia had already taken the steps she had, and thanks to the snags that had kept her "stalled" in place at times, she was in a perfect position to say yes to the new opportunity. It proved to be a joyful move for her and her family in all ways. Her careful work with the sensitivity that initially prompted her to jump out of the crises as fast as possible transmuted into joy when the right solution appeared. Some patience as well as practice with her extremely sensitive nature served her well in the long run.

The Spectrum of Sensitivity

Clearly, our bodies come with built-in receptivity to the environment. Not only the heat of the sun, the wetness of rain, or the smell of roses, but the emotional climate around us is constantly taken in and processed. We all are impacted differently by these conditions: there is clearly a continuum of human sensitivity. Within that spectrum is a group of highly sensitive individuals, some of whom have been identified by way of a Highly Sensitive Person questionnaire, and tested using functional magnetic resonance imaging. Distinct neural differences were demonstrated in the sensory processing regions of their brains, especially in the visual areas. Along with an increase in brain activation, there is a significantly slower response time in sensitive people. Apparently the overload of input causes the sensitive person to think about what to do longer than less sensitive individuals.[1]

In the population of those who test as highly sensitive there is a high incidence of introversion as well as clinically diagnosed neurotic behavior. The behavioral attributes of these people include being bothered by intense stimuli. They startle easily and are affected strongly by pain and hurry-up pressure. The highly sensitive person tunes into other's moods rapidly and accurately. In that regard they have the capacity to be highly empathetic. While they notice subtle details of any place, they also pick up and process the subtle qualities of people. This area of research underscores how differently each of us perceive the world based on the biology of the brain and sensory organs.

Some current research on how we experience smells underscores the uniqueness of individual reality. We have about 400 olfactory receptors and the associated genetic codes that shape each one. The variations in those codes are such that you may smell flowers but I experience, well, stale urine. Since our individual genetics directly relate to perception in this case, you and I could never agree on what we smell. Biology trumps our olfactory reality.[2]

A separate but intriguing area of research examines a rare condition in which the subject lacks the ability to recognize faces. Those who cannot remember a face when there is no brain damage or other defects have a condition called developmental prosopagnosia. Oliver Sacks writes beautifully in *The Mind's Eye* about this syndrome from his personal experience.[3] There are also individuals who are far on the opposite end of the spectrum—the super recognizers. Many of these individuals have to change their communication style because they can't go around greeting everyone who looks familiar. Imagine someone approaching you at your local coffee shop and cheerily saying that they saw you at a football game three years prior. You might think you were being stalked.[4]

We can't do anything about the biology of the neurons we inherit nor how they connect or don't connect with each other. We can, however, understand how experience shapes the interpretation of what we perceive. People in my office speak about their sensitivity to energy, to images, sounds, and touch that is far outside the ordinary. Vivid colors swirl, shift, and sparkle like fireworks in their mind when their eyes are closed. An array of beautiful purple, green, or blue color floods their inner vision. They report the aroma of roses, soft music, or a sense of shivery wind that sweeps through their body. There is no rational explanation for these phenomena. Some welcome the occurrence as a blessing. Others frame the experience as too weird and, on the whole, frightening. They ask me to get rid of their sensitivity. To do that would be the equivalent of blinding someone because the glare of full sunlight is uncomfortable. A better approach would be sunglasses and instruction on how to use them.

TUNE IN TO RESONANCE

If you ever feel overwhelmed, find a cozy place in your home where you can curl up with a comforter or blanket. Imagine some lovely folding screens that have graceful and rather magical qualities that filter out any input that would distress you. The screens are sturdy yet transparent to the best energy for you. You have access to any number of these folding screens depending on your level of sensitivity. In your mind place several around you to give you shielding. You might place them around your bathtub if you prefer a warm soak. Enjoy the safety of your special location with a flow of energy that supports and heals you.

Decision Making for Sensitive People

How do we know what is real and how to evaluate what seems overwhelming? Maybe we've made choices that did not work out well, or were disastrous and led us to live fearfully. Others just do not understand how inundated a sensitive person can become when they see or otherwise experience so much more phenomena than anyone around them. The coping mechanism of avoidance can lead to isolation and that becomes unhealthy in so many ways. For me, discernment became an antidote to isolation, and a tool for survival. Through it, in fact, I found joy in having a sensitive nature.

Here are some simple steps to craft a discernment process. Honor your logical mind, and look at the issue with the intent to frame a question. The next step is to refine your question. Taking time to journal can be helpful to summarize the information that seems most relevant and to write out the question as it evolved with your process. There is an "enough already" moment when the logical mind has done its work. Then contemplation takes over. As you go deeper and allow the thought processes to settle into the background, open yourself to a solution that may come in unbidden ways. As you tap your inner resources, remain alert to a dream or an unexpected insight that may occur at the most unanticipated time.

One of the things I hear most often from very sensitive people is that they have a difficult time making decisions. In part this is based on all the input they receive. The following is offered as a way to assist with the process.

TUNE IN TO RESONANCE

Relax into the sensitive aspects of yourself without judgment or restriction. Know that each bit of data and awareness has value. In your mind's image, see a pile of papers that contain, sheet by sheet, statements about the information you have acquired.

Imagine that you have three containers in front of you. Place the data you don't need in one. Place the data that is high priority in another. In the third container, place those bits that you are not sure about. Now is the time to make the hypothetical decision. Select the high priority bin and use it. Know that extraneous input has been sorted out, and you do not need to be overwhelmed by it. You have additional information, should it become necessary, in that third bin. Let the decision be complete and trust yourself.

How about standing up and doing a dance for joy in proceeding through the discernment process using your logical mind, exercising choice, and honoring your sensitive nature? You can flourish in the world and honor your sensitivity.

The short version is: think, pause, turn within, trust, act.

Sensitivity is a Gift

How did the ultra sensitive label get started? What would it take to drop the belief that sensitivity is wrong? The more aware we are, the more intensely those incoming sensations impact us. Soon the label of overly sensitive becomes an established identity. Those closest to us may attach that label when exasperated at how long we take to make a decision or how we jump at loud sounds. We make our associates uncomfortable.

As we grow spiritually, we naturally become more sensitive. Meditation changes not only brain function toward enhanced awareness but it increases the urge to assist those who are suffering. Using fMRI scans that response can be seen in specific areas of the brain that are activated by someone else's pain. If we were not already ultra sensitive, we'd grow closer to that state as we meditated. Compassion arises and our emotional responses become stronger.

Sandra was a highly educated woman with a doctorate in engineering. She relied on her ever-so-rational mind, tight logic, and unemotional response to all the complicated tasks that were part of her career. That style of thinking and living had become her way of being in all aspects of life. It worked well for her until she had an encounter with spirituality. Her life changed as a spontaneous awakening brought visions, sensations, and insights she never dreamed possible. She became far more emotionally responsive. The challenge for her in her new state of being included many physical issues and symptoms.

Her body had one ache, pain, or problem after the other. She tried many intuitive readers and read books but had no relief for her symptoms. When she was in the presence of spiritual people, individually or at a conference, she might shake, twitch, or shudder at inopportune times and without conscious control. This was more than disconcerting to Sandra. How could she navigate her life without full control? In particular, what was the tremor in her legs and feet all about? Her doctor could not find evidence of Parkinson's disease; although, the trembling certainly looked suspicious. This shaking was much more pronounced in situations where she was in touch with her spirituality. I met her at my office for a session; she had flown to Seattle from Philadelphia to attend a conference. Comfortably seated on the gray leather couch, she showed no signs of tremors anywhere in her body. Her hands, feet, and legs were perfectly still as she told me her history and her amazement at how her life had changed. She also spoke about her frustration with her "symptoms" and that she had no convincing answers from all the sources she had consulted. When it was time for healing work, she kicked off her shoes and climbed onto my treatment table. The minute her body relaxed and settled into the cushioned surface, her legs started unmistakably shaking. She moved a lot, sometimes rolling from side to side. At one point she turned over and assumed the yoga position known as prayer pose. Eventually she returned to lying on her back as we had started and her body grew quiet, peaceful, and still. As with all my clients, near the end of the session, I left the room and gave her time to rest before getting up. When I returned we had a lot to talk about. Sandra felt that she had had an excellent experience and felt good physically. We talked for some time about the various sensations that inundated her body. While the shaking was strongest, she also had a display of bright and beautiful colors that filled her inner vision. By the time we were finished, her body was calm and still. Her face was glowing and radiant. She wrote to me about a week after the session: "It was so life affirming to walk out of a healing session feeling good and seeing a way forward. That has not happened for me for a long time."

Her story reminded me of some of the early parts of my own spiritual journey. Early in my transition from scientist to healing facilitator, I met Fred Pankratz, one of those people who seems to show up at exactly the right time and place. Fred had been a contractor in Alaska and a frequent traveler to the Philippines where he was considered a holy man by locals in the countryside near Mount Banáhao, a half-day's drive from Manila. Fred also spent time in Seattle where I met him through a mutual friend. When Fred did healing sessions for me in those early days I would start shaking uncontrollably. I could not predict when the phenomenon would start nor could I turn it off at will. Fred patiently coached me to relax into the movement and instructed me to increase my meditation practice in the days that followed the session. His explanation was that my body needed to adapt to the increase in energy that now coursed through it. It is important to know that we can work with the energy of resonant union so that the body is not subject to shaking, twitching, shouting, or weeping at inopportune moments. The practice at the conclusion of this chapter gives some suggestions for how to engage this energy and not have it overpower the body.

What is that energy? The closest I've come to an answer that is the theme of this book. There is a resonance that the physical body is able to make with something so far beyond our most able science that we can only call it the Mystery. When the body and Mystery unite directly, the body reacts. Religious traditions have named the resonant connection in various ways: Kundalini (Hindu); unexpected blessing (Catholic); Satori, Samadhi, Shakti, Chi, Mahamudra, Dzogchen (various types of Buddhism and Hinduism); fana (Sufism); mukti (Sikhism); and mystical union (Christian mysticism) to name a few. Whatever name is given for this state of consciousness, the descriptions of ecstasy, bliss, and overwhelming compassion are similar regardless of culture or religion. Isn't it astounding that we can resonate with a power greater than ourselves and that the result of that resonance is able to ignite the soul? Undeniably, the resonance of union produces profound joy. Our inborn sensitive nature can lead us there, as can our expanded sensitivity when we engage spiritual practice. Here is where we find a type of joy that bubbles up from inside and is not dependent on outer circumstances. The only way I've found to tap that wellspring is through spiritual practice. There has not been one and only one all-inclusive practice for me. Each sunrise brings a new opportunity and challenge to balance, to harmonize, to appreciate, to find clarity, to meet the unique day by adapting known resources and discovering new ones. Not that long ago I woke without my usual sense of great joy. Day after day this heavyheartedness persisted and I could not shake the heaviness of suffering I had absorbed. The solution was not to dismiss the suffering or to sit through five comedies. The solution was to increase my connection of union with the Mystery. To do that I extended my meditation time and shifted my practice to allow for more silence and thereby, I could show up for the blessing of mystical union. I was not disappointed.

RESONANCE

Sensitivity is a gift, not a curse. Joy is the cue that you have allowed your sensitive nature to resonate with the Mystery and that you have found an authentic spiritual connection.

THE PRACTICE: SENSITIVITY AND JOY

You can become a human rheostat for healing energy and spiritual energy that enters your body. The essence of a physical rheostat is a switch within a circuit that allows variations in how much current comes through without losing contact with the source.

Maybe it is one of those particular days when you feel sensitive to every nuance and therefore emotionally vulnerable. You feel as if you are on overload—or a fraction away from overload. Stop for a few minutes and find your breath. Slow down a bit. Follow your slower breath. Ask your spiritual guides (assume that you have one or more whether you know them or not) to gently turn down the energy flow at the intersection of your body and spirit. Imagine that you can touch a dimmer switch and adjust the intensity of spiritual energy running through your body. Find a setting that is most comfortable for this instant in time. You can change the setting, up or down, whenever you choose. If you are meditating and start to have some physical symptom such as shaking that is uncomfortable, use your rheostat to adjust the energy.

If you are a healing facilitator for someone else, pay close attention to what is the right amount of energy for them. Adjust the "current" so that it feels compatible with what they need and does not overload them. A blast of maximum output is not necessarily healing. A flow of optimum energy is much better.

Lastly, send a burst of appreciation for your innate sensitivity and for the expansion of your awareness through spiritual practice. Relax into the joy that is deeply native to your soul.

CHAPTER 9

RESONANCE AND TRANSFORMATION

*The way of the Creative works through change
and transformation, so that each thing receives its
true nature and destiny and comes into permanent
accord with the Great Harmony.*

— ALEXANDER POPE

The old woman with wise eyes, shrewd glances, and hair so long that it touched the backs of her knees says, "I will take you to an empowerment temple for our own healers. You will do a ceremony as we do."

I don't want to appear overly eager but I could jump up and run down the narrow dusty street shouting with joy. After 12 weeks in Bali, this is a connection to an authentic part of the healing culture I've longed to experience. Plans are formed and agreements made about the time to gather for the drive to the healer's temple. We discuss what kind of offerings to bring and who will drive us. I can hardly wait for the next day when we will embark on the journey of initiation. I feel so at home and resonant with the island of Bali and with this particular healer, Jero Mangku. Before this trip, I had been satisfied with my work and my life, but now I felt restlessness. It was time to expand and break out of the confines of my current level of consciousness.

Morning comes and we gather at Jero's home. Jero is dressed in a fine sarong, with a temple scarf tied at her waist. Her hair is freshly twined high atop her head. Jero's husband, often the gracious host, server of coffee and fruits, is today splendidly dressed in priest's attire and carries a tray of offerings ready for the gods. My translator, Budi, is ready and able as always but somewhat quieter than usual. I ask him privately if he knows where the temple is located and whether he has been there before. He assures me that he has, but some quiver in his voice, some slight avoidance of my gaze, some stoop to his shoulders indicates uncertainty. The driver, one I have not met before, formally opens the car door for Jero, and she settles into the front seat. He slips in behind the wheel and the rest of us squeeze into the back together. Off we go.

Through the outskirts of Denpasar, capital city of Bali, we slowly proceed, stopping at a small outdoor market to pick up additional flowers for the offering baskets. Everything is heated by the equatorial sun, close and hot. Trees, people, and market wares exude perfumed oils. Essence of spice, essence of heat, essence of flowers, essence of dust, essence of color, and the essence of intensity mingle in the soft touch of ocean wind. They foretell the coming initiation but I cannot get the flavor of their story. I cannot understand their soft whisper, nor see the form to come.

The mirage shimmers into patterns that flow away too fast. The car is moving again, and we are headed out to the main road that will take us North.

After an hour's drive we turn down a narrow, unmarked road. The asphalt surface is no longer smooth but crumbled into pits. The car slows markedly as we climb into and out of one pothole after another. Budi is very quiet. His usual chatty, gregarious self has buckled into an unfamiliar silence. He speaks softly to me, "I do not know this temple."

Chills of fear run up my spine. I have no reply. I begin to entertain an unsettling thought: *I could die out here and no one would know where to find my remains. I am completely at the mercy of the goodwill, not only of my companions, but of the gods of life and death.* I had thought that my near-death experience had completely purged me of any fear of death, but I realize that was not totally true.

We cross numerous deep jungle gorges with rushing rivers below with only the support of plank board bridges. I notice how quiet everyone becomes when we encounter a bridge. Jero's husband whispers to me, "Notice what she does when we are in the middle of the bridge." As we approached the next gorge I looked at Jero. Suddenly her back jerks stiffly upright, her right hand covers her chest, and she mouths silent words. When our tires leave the planks, she relaxes, simply riding along once again.

No one chats on this trip. It is not a social outing. No picnic basket was packed; no jug of lemonade was prepared. Rising out of my thoughts and worries, I smell sea-air and lean forward to look past the driver's head. There are black sand beaches, palm trees, and an ocean that shimmers in the distance. Our car trip ends in a dusty pullover. We pile out, and I notice chunks of black pumice and lava pebbles scattered on the ground that had been spewed out by Mount Agung, when it last erupted in the late 1960s. In Bali it seems that there are always people, a small village, or a few family dwellings on every road. Notably, in this place there are no people, no priests, nor groundskeepers that look after this temple. There are no other cars or buildings of any kind.

Silently, we troop along behind Jero to the gate of the healer's empowerment temple. Very directly, Jero walks through the split gate that represents the threshold between sacred and secular, and the split of the dualistic mind. She sits on the steps that lead to the whole gate, which represents the prepared, undivided mind. She gestures for me to sit in the dirt at the base of the steps. She lights incense, prays, and sprinkles holy water on the offerings arranged on a gilded plate. She leads me in a prayer and purification ritual which includes the required sprinkling with holy water from the petals of a plumeria flower dipped in a small vessel of blessed water.

Jero speaks. "The god of the temple accepts our offerings and accepts Joyce. Proceed."

We follow her to a side court. We pass under an archway into a dark shrine. It feels as though we have walked into a place that could not be entered or even physically seen without permission from the temple gods. Jero sits in front of the shrine on some steps and motions for me to take my place again in the dust of the ground below her. She repeats her chants and offerings. Smoke billows from a cluster of incense sticks and rises to the carved god of the shrine, a visage I have not seen before in Bali or anywhere else.

The statue is about five feet tall, dark, with a narrow somewhat human but mostly otherworldly face. This was not a familiar deity as seen on many Balinese statues of

Shiva, Ganesha, or other gods. The stones that surround the statue are dark and seem very old. Some chunks have broken away and were restacked with care, but not with mortar. Jungle vegetation curls around the shrine from a green place behind. Tendrils reach for the god's arms, legs, and brow. Jero completes her chants and pulls me to stand, takes my hands, opens my arms as wide as they can go. She begins to dance, swirls, dips, and spins ever so fast. I dance with her as a joyful spirit buoys my awareness. As she finishes her dance, she declares that the god of the temple welcomes us and is pleased with us being there, and, furthermore, accepts me and my vocation as a healer. From this descent into the depths both literally and metaphorically, we move deeper into the temple grounds. Glistening in the sun is an enormous pool of water, fed by a fresh water spring. The sides of the pool are formed of stone that make a rectangular container for this unexpected source of clear water. The ledge above the pool is wide enough to walk upon. At one end the ledge juts out into the pool forming a walkway to a small shrine. Jero proceeds across by herself and sets up an offering at the base of the shrine. At some subtle signal, her husband walks around me, takes my hands in his, and leads me out to the shrine. Jero motions for me to sit down and then begins a lovely chant. The air is sweet here, the sun is refreshing, and the pool dazzles the eyes. My eyes close as my spirit lifts, drifts upward along with the smoke from the incense.

Jero's voice shifts from a deep, measured intonation to a higher pitch, a more uneven sound. Her face is different and her head is thrown back. The shaman in her appears. She looks like a lioness. Her long hair is still physically fixed in its tight bun, but it seems to be a mane flowing with magnificence. I lean forward to catch all the energy of her being and to hear her speak. She begins with words that sound like thunder. Budi translates: "Joyce, you are welcome and accepted by generations of healers and the deities that protect them. Furthermore you must wash only in Lux soap and dust with powder."

Lux soap! What is this? Here I am waiting for a life-changing message, and I'm told to wash in some smelly pink soap. Everyone is deadpan serious, and I can hardly keep from bursting into giggles. At first I am figuring that Lux means light in Latin and there is a hidden message here, but that plainly does not resonate. I abandon all hope of understanding this whole event as we all traipse out to the car with curiously happy hearts. On one hand, I am puzzled by the oddly incongruent message, but on the other hand, I feel as light as if I were walking on air. Even thought I cannot make sense of the soap message, I am unconcerned as the blessing of the whole experience is deep at work within me.

Back in the car, we head out of the strangely abandoned temple site. We approach the first bridge and the car slowly eases onto the creaking wood. Jero sits stiffly upright and flurries of words pour out. She finishes and drops back into the seat. Budi translates immediately. The gist of the message was one of encouragement for my work as a healing facilitator, profound blessing on the journey my life would take, and a joyful acknowledgement of the genuineness of the calling. All this came at a point when I had been overwhelmed with doubt about changing careers and my suitability as a healer. The timeliness of Jero's message was comforting and settled my concern. Later, as I developed a steady meditation practice, the doubt and uncertainty dissolved altogether. Resonance was the key to my connection with Jero. Transformation was the required shift I needed to make to progress in my life and my work. Those shifts may come with quiet changes in awareness. However, when I've been most strongly stuck in my life, the agent of change has also been more powerful.

The encouraging message from Jero was important and welcome, but the actual test was to sustain the experience of lightness or the heightened feeling of compassion that the ceremony produced. Messages are wonderful but the essence is not the spoken words, it is in the unspoken and nonconceptual occurrence. It is the inner experience that carries the teaching. It has taken me many years since the Bali sojourn to understand that truth. I had looked for words or actions to make the difference. Now I am aware of the experience of blessing that supersedes any communication or any deed.

Shamans refresh with holy water
Ordinary reality tangible hope
Simple tasks and simple forms
Peel bananas bubble rice pots
Recall tales that now make sense
Spirit pulls relentlessly
Exhaustion grasps surprising meaning
Rocks and wind fully audible
I stumble into dance
My mumbling turns to song
Goodness blesses who I am
Transformed beyond imagination

TUNE IN TO RESONANCE

Consider the times of growth in your life. What prompted them? Was it difficult or easy to make the changes you needed? How are you different now than you were before you changed? Take a moment to appreciate the agents of change whether kind and considerate or difficult and demanding. In another moment generate gratitude for yourself, your response to the situations and people, and your own unique process of growth.

Resonance That Leads to Transformation

Not everyone needs to sit at the feet of a shaman in front of strange statues to find a route to transformation. But we do need to find ways to free ourselves from restrictive beliefs and from stuck places. We must find the deep inner resonance that connects us with the life-giving essence within and with that which is greater than ourselves.

There are many teachers, authors, and speakers who can inform you as to how they found their transformative path. They have taught it to others who found it to be inspiring and who then followed that path with rapt attention and in detail. I've talked to many former followers as clients who recall with anger and sadness how carefully they pursued each instruction and nuance. Yet they eventually came to a sense of despair and meaninglessness. The question is either *What did I do wrong?* or *How could I have been so deceived?*

I've come to think of the myriad voices out there that have *the* answer, as voices that found *their* answer. I can learn from their insights and honor their teachings if some part resonates with me. We can take what works and leave the rest. If you are at a friend's house for dinner and one of the dishes includes sautéed green peppers and you are allergic to green peppers, do you eat them anyway? Or do you enjoy the other foods and not partake of the one that would send you to the emergency room? At some point, we got conditioned to believe that we have to take the whole package of any belief system. In the long run, it is far better to use your own judgment and discern bit by bit what is resonant with your inner truth.

So then, how do any of us find inner truth and discern the resonant from the dissonant? One major means to discernment is the process of learning to trust your emotions. Well over a decade ago I wrote these words in my journal: "I know if I veer from my guidance that I feel terrible—become deeply unhappy and feel estranged from myself and from Spirit." Over the years, the process has become more and more fine-tuned, as I discovered that the guidance was for my highest good and exquisitely reliable. The guidance is the presence of a mysterious love that holds the best for each of us in our journey through this lifetime and, perhaps, many lifetimes. To break loose of myopic vision and truly see oneself and the universe; to receive blessings in near or far-away temples, or within the temple of the heart, and know that love abides with us forever is invaluable. I suspect that this is why we are here. It is more about being than about doing any specific thing during our multitude of rotations around the sun.

Resonance with Place

There are places where we feel something that reminds us that we had been there before, whether in this lifetime or another. I did not believe in past lives until I had the near-death experience and I returned with a unambiguous knowing that I had lived before and would live again. This all became clearer when I traveled to the Philippines and worked with a healer in the mountain city of Baguio for three months. We would drive to various places for ceremony or to visit someone. On more than one occasion

I would look out the window of the car and see a natural feature of the environment—a grassy knoll, or a cluster of trees, or a stream, and have an instantaneous knowing that I had been there before. Not only been there, but had a major life event or spiritual awakening at that very spot. The feeling was intense. Each time I would gasp involuntarily, and it would take a minute for me to catch my breath. I felt that my chest had been compressed as if by a shock wave. This was not only about the recognition of place, but that an estranged part of me was ready for integration. That part was not split off in this lifetime nor was it caused by some trauma. I consider it a part of my soul that was not accessible. Others speak of soul retrieval—one of those ideas that cannot be proven by scientific means, but once it happens, even a linear, logical mind has to consider the possibility. What if we were healers in another life and acquired skills that could reunite with the conscious mind once awakened? Is it possible that a strong resonance with place promotes such an awakening and we become more whole? There is a yearning inside of us for connection just as cells in our body connect constantly with each other. If 100 trillion cells reach for their neighbor, why shouldn't we reach for the fullness of our own being?

In a spiritual sense, the perception of aspects of one's personal universe that return by way of some sort of soul retrieval is astounding. The universe now exists in a larger and more tangible form. How much of the fullness of the universe do we not perceive? How gripping a thought that we may be able to find aspects of soul and, therefore, aspects of self that have been hidden heretofore. What don't we remember about who we are, or how we were before taking on a human form? Visions and feelings we may have during meditation practice or during a near-death experience are perhaps a sampler of what we have forgotten at a soul level.

At a more practical level, I hear comments from people who move to Seattle that run the gamut. "I came for a visit and did not plan to stay, but now I've been here for three years and cannot imagine living anywhere else. I love it here." Others say, "I hate this place. How can you stand living here?" Each place has its own resonance, and our work is to notice whether we are in harmony or disharmony with the place we've chosen rather than to try and force a perfect fit. We may be able to make adjustments—live in a different neighborhood in the city—or we may have to pack up and move. I've lived in Seattle for more than 30 years and love it. However, when the muse moves me, I head for a wilderness spot in the Cascade Mountains. This place had a creative resonance for me from the first ski trip decades ago. Some friends came here and actually purchased a cabin. Much to their consternation, they detested the place, and sold as soon as they realized how much it did not work for them. It is valuable to develop your own sense of resonance with place and to continue to extend that into deeper and more subtle senses. It saves us time and effort and deepens our trust in our innate abilities.

Tune In to Resonance

Current neurological research indicates that when we remember a place or event with attention to detail that the same neurons become active that would if we were there in real time. If the memory is a trauma, it is relived, and if the memory is a good one, we are blessed once again.

Think of a place where you felt especially light and happy. In particular, recall a place where you felt spiritually connected in the best possible way. Your inner sense was expansive, at peace, and joyful. You felt a splendid quiet that goes beyond description. Imagine that you can be there in that place in the present moment. Ask what gifts are there for you now. With each breath you can embrace those gifts and allow them to integrate with clarity into your conscious mind. It is not necessary to know exactly what may have changed for you right away, but be aware of your responses to everyday situations. You may find that you respond with more compassion, with less angst, and with quicker resolution to problems that occur.

When you remember those places that are uplifting, you can return there over and over again in your mind. They can become sacred places for renewal. They are also a setting for you to take a next step in transformation.

Resonance with People

The relationships we have with each other are complex to say the least. There is family to start. Most mothers, with the help of those hormones that surge at the time of giving birth, feel closeness with their baby that is surprisingly intense in a loving and protective way. It is a peak experience for mom, and it sets us up for close connections later in life.

What about the neurology that came packed in our skulls at birth? More and more evidence points to the wiring of the brain that contributes to, if not causes, some severe disorders. Exactly how that neural circuitry develops is not known, but certain deficiencies in it apparently generate psychopathic behavior.

We can be grateful for what genetic gifts we do have and for the efficacious expression of those genes. How do we make the most of what we have? A smart and sensitive woman had a telephone session with me. She had left a lucrative position as an attorney in a major firm in Chicago to take a job on the East coast with a philanthropic organization. She had a deep commitment to use her talents to help others and looked to the new job to fully engage her skills and in so doing enable a sense of meaningfulness to her life. To her dismay she found that her colleagues were very difficult to work with. Her direct manager treated her disrespectfully and rather brutally. When a project that the manager was responsible for was not finished, she dumped it on my client and required that she work an entire weekend to cover for her boss's poor performance. My client had wanted to use her gifts, to make the most of them, and she was stuck in a situation that was far different than she had anticipated. Although her intention was clear and admirable, the people at this agency were not a good fit. That disharmony can change—or not. How much time should we devote to the "hang in there" phase? How often do we hear "I wish I had left years ago, I had no idea how much this has taken out of me." And sometimes just the opposite is true; "I am so glad that I stuck it out. I grew, I learned to communicate better, and things have worked out much better than I expected."

Not only in work situations, but in personal relationships the quality of initial connection is important and informative. We have all heard about two people who saw each other "across a crowded room," fell in love instantly, and remained googly-eyed lovers 25 years later. Few of us have been so fortunate as to experience that kind of connection in our first relationships. We may find that we grow at different rates or in different ways, or we may discover irreconcilable differences with a partner. Perhaps an astute counselor can help bring us into harmony again, or help us see that the relationship is complete and finished. Living systems such as ourselves always change. When we are able to embrace the change that comes into our lives and relationships, to flow harmoniously with what is, then the power of transformation can be manifest for us.

TUNE IN TO RESONANCE

If there is a person in your life with whom you have challenges, worries, or deep love, here is a simple practice. Visualize them a few feet in front of you and surround them with a flowing spiral of golden light. Let this be with the simple intention of support for their highest good. Allow this to stop the flow of worry energy or consternation that you have been holding in relation to them. Note how this practice works for you and how it transforms the dynamic between you and the other.

This practice of "spirals of light" is one that I do regularly and have found to be exceptionally effective. The foundational requirement is that we become neutral as we visualize the energy going to the person. That neutrality may blossom into unconditional compassion; although, rest assured that is not required.

Resonance with Practice

Your bookshelf may have a cluster of books on meditation, and you may have listened to CDs and speakers who present any number of ways to achieve that promised land of the meditative mind. This very book you are now holding has practices throughout and detailed instructions that accompany each couplet chapter. The purpose of those suggested meditations is to give you a variety of models that you can adapt for your own practice. In order to fully use them and make them your own, notice which ones light up for you. Here we are at resonance again. That feeling of lift, that catch-in-the-breath, that sense of possibility for blessing is the outcome you seek.

Jon recently came to my office for a session looking woebegone. His face was a pasty gray; his shoulders slumped. He had certain physical challenges and medical appointments in the near future, and he had an overwhelming sense of overload in his life. Members of his family were in the midst of severe difficulties and lived far away, so he felt powerless to help them. A problem faced him everywhere he turned, and there was no relief in sight. Jon valued the spiritual side of life and had tried every suggested style of meditation that his library of books offered. He followed every voice on his CDs, but nothing worked for him. By the time we met, he had abandoned any kind of practice and felt that he was a self-help dropout. Jon desperately wanted a way to calm himself when he felt overwhelmed, and a way to connect to the healing energy that he experienced during our sessions.

I do not have a one-size-fits-all or standard practice for myself or anyone else. The following questions may help you find the places, people and practices that best serve you.

Where do you feel the most relaxed and open to support?

If that place is out of doors, and it is reasonable to do so, go to the beach or to a park where tall trees grow, or go for a walk so you can move and breathe fresh air. If you are a runner, run. If the weather is conducive after you've walked or run, find a place to sit for a while and let your mind become quiet and your breath deep and slow. If thoughts come up do not fight them; simply return your awareness to the breath. Stay with the breath in the present moment for as long as you can and without any desire for anything in particular. Relax into the quiet of your inner self and rest there as long as it feels good. If your good place is at home or in a church, temple, or synagogue, go there and do the same as you sit in the quiet sanctuary. Your place might be at home with soft music, a cup of tea, or sequestered in a calm corner, on a couch, or cushion. Setting aside a small place for the practice of meditation can strengthen your experience, as each time you go there you are reminded of your intention to slow down and turn within. Just as a bed reminds you and supports you to sleep, a separate and dedicated place speaks to you of meditation. If you use a wheelchair or happen to be in a hospital, meditation is equally available to you.

What is the most comfortable body position for you to maintain for 5 to 30 minutes?

It is not necessary to sit cross-legged to practice. You can sit with your legs stretched out in front of you, propped up on pillows, or supported in your favorite chair, or even lying down, if needed. Be sure you are warm enough. I have a yak wool blanket that is soft and cozy warm. I love to imagine that it can transport me to the steppes of Tibet where I can gaze at Mount Kailash, a holy place. Do not worry about the time you spend. Three minutes of deep quiet is a great place to begin. The next day it may become ten minutes, and one day you may lose all track of time, and surprise yourself with the delight of being cradled in effortless blessing and spiritual support.

Have you had a practice in the past that made your heart happy?

Use a familiar practice to begin. As your meditation develops, allow the formal style to slowly melt away, and go deeper into silence. If you became bored with a particular way of meditating let that be a signal to enter the gate of exploration. Allow methods to drop away as you trust your inner guidance to take you deeper into the heart of ultimate existence, consciousness, and bliss.

Are there sounds, chants, or songs that lift your spirit?

You can begin your practice time with mantra, prayer, chant, or song as an interlude between all the busyness of ordinary reality, and the altered state of consciousness that meditation unlocks. Be careful not to require yourself to perform a certain number of repetitions, but to let the prayer slowly cease as you enter a state of quietness. You may find that the Mystery is undeniably a mystery and the exploration of the unknown territory within you is the ultimate adventure—the hero's journey.

Is there a particular religion or philosophy that speaks the most clearly or deeply to you?

For some there is a distinct path of approach to the mystery of the universe. If that is the case for you, please honor and enjoy the blessing of your resonant faith. It surely can lead you to growth and transformation. If you have explored several religions and they all have gifted you with an aspect of growth, how superb. You can use all that you have learned and experienced as a foundation. Are you ready for your own expedition to enhanced awareness, serenity, and compassionate consciousness? The classic journey of the hero begins with the finding of the right companions, the attainment of skills, the discovery of a "weapon" of power, and the courage to face all that appears on the path. Perhaps this is the time for you to see yourself as the hero of your story.

THE PRACTICE: RESONANCE AND TRANSFORMATION

Glance back at the questions we just covered and let them guide you to a good place, posture, style, and pattern for this unique day and moment in the day for practice. There is no previous time just like this one, and there will be no time in the future exactly like this one. Right now is a universe unto itself, and you are central to the moment. Your breath reminds you that you are alive, you are conscious, you are blessed.

Ask that the most transformative connection possible link you to a higher power and carry you gently to new levels of resonance and growth. You may wish to imagine what it would feel like to climb aboard the broad back of a giant eagle, take to the sky, and ask Great Spirit to soar with you. Float on the wind of spirit.

When you return to everyday perception, take time to notice what may have changed during your exploration. It is important that each new stride integrate in your life in positive ways. Healing is available to you directly with this practice as the touch of spirit brings renewal, vitality, and health.

CONCLUSION

The moments of our lives pass quickly when we are absorbed in the details of work, home, family, and particularly when there are health concerns. We often yearn for and seek a sense of well-being and a safe haven from the challenges of our busy lives. In the midst of all of this, the nine paired qualities we've explored in this book reside within us. They are not separate from us. Their resonance is an aspect of our basic and essential self. Each pair ignites the divine spark of our most basic and true self. As you practice each of the suggested couplets, I trust that you will tap into additional qualities. Allow your wisdom-self to experience the interface between consciousness and Mystery. As you live at that place, you may surprise yourself when you wake up giggling, or know what your loved one's next sentence is before it is spoken.

Such spontaneous gifts of the spirit come from the same place of silence and Mystery that is within you and connects you to the oneness of everything. Each chapter title, each couplet, came to me from that place during meditation. I encourage you to work with the couplets that resonate most strongly for you. Allow that harmony to awaken new dimensions of your true self.

A SIMPLE GUIDE
TO CELL BIOLOGY

There are approximately 200 different cell types in the body, each with a unique job to do, yet almost all cells share some key features. An understanding of basic cell biology can assist us in directing healing energy to the body, as it helps to answer the question, "What is the science of the situation?"

IPAC – The Four Keys to Cell Function

Information, Power, Action, and Communication allow the cells in our bodies to keep us alive, and by using the IPAC mnemonic you can keep these functions in mind without needing to memorize lots of scientific terms.

Information in a cell is primarily retained in the nucleus. This structure in the cell interior contains thousands of strands of DNA, the codes that hold the blueprints for every part of the human body. You may have seen images of the exquisite double-helix structure of DNA, but unless a cell is in the process of dividing, these strands are usually unwound and busy directing a cell's individual work.

Within each strand of DNA are individual genes, or code groups, that hold the keys to how a cell operates. But not all genes are expressing at any given time. Certain proteins associated with a gene grouping can keep it from being active. There are also large sections of DNA that don't seem to code for anything. These sections have been called "junk DNA," but recent work has shown that this DNA controls how genes function.[1]

In your work to promote health for yourself and others, it is important to know that the information part of the cells is not static, it's not cut and dried. Gene expression can be turned on or off and is influenced by many factors both internally and externally. As much as we now know about DNA, and how genes operate, remember that much more is still a mystery. Allow both the science and the mystery to inform your healing practice.

Power in our cells is provided by the subcellular part— the mitochondrial DNA. For everything we do at the cellular level and at the body level, we need power. Cells require power to create enzymes, hormones, and other products needed by the body. Muscles require power to facilitate movement. The mitochondria store and release energy as it is needed within a cell. Every cell in your body has hundreds and hundreds of these power packs.

These battery packs each have a special enzyme that can capture, store, and release energy as needed by the cell. A tiny, armlike projection is an integral part of that enzyme (ATPase), and it spins around when the mitochondria are working to provide energy. These whirly-gigs churn out power for all that we do.

Vitality resides in every part of your body, it is tangible and systematically woven into every tiny cellular structure within you. Feel the whir of the power within and know that without any conscious effort on your part all the power you need is spinning in every cell right now.

Action takes place in a cellular structure called the endoplasmic reticulum. This is the manufacturing plant within each cell, where the molecules needed for life are created. Each cell has layer upon layer of these ER membranes working away. All this happens through the direction of the cell's DNA with the help of the power coming from the mitochondria. Each cell is capable of producing many different substances, but often a cell type is biased in its operation by the organ type in which it resides. Specific cells in the pancreas produce insulin and other metabolic enzymes, while muscle cells produce myosin and actin that slide back and forth to produce the action needed for proper muscle operation. Immune system cells produce substances that help to seek out, control, and destroy invaders to the body.

Communication is vital to every aspect of cell life and death. The outer membrane of a cell can communicate directly with the cells around it through touch, by sending out nanotubes that carry bio-chemical messages to nearby cells. Sometimes cells communicate by releasing their products into the bloodstream. In this way they can communicate with cells in another part of the body. Communication also happens internally in a cell. The DNA communicates to the action centers, and the action centers are physically associated to the power packs.

The world of our cells is alive with nonstop communication which allows each cell and cell group to maintain proper balance in all that is required both for production and power. Healing work is, in essence, communication. Allow your innate ability to communicate at this very deep level to inform your healing journey. Choose helpful communications that honor and respect the remarkable capacities of the body. You assist the body in maintaining balance and harmony when the mental messages you hold are compassionate and peaceful.

Major Cell Types

Bone – The outer, inorganic part of bone is calcium phosphate, a piezo-electric crystal. Electrons flow within these crystalline structures when we bear weight and the bone itself also deforms slightly during this action. The flow of electrons is healthy for the bone as it prompts calcium deposits to align properly along an organic collagen matrix. Two integral bone cell types that are useful in healing are osteoclasts and osteoblasts. The former can remove bone structure and the latter replace bone structure.

Muscle – This tissue is primarily composed of two types of protein fiber—myosin and actin. The fibers slide across one another to flex and extend the muscles. This tissue is rich with blood vessels that bring nutrients and remove the by-products of exertion. Muscles work every time you wiggle your ears, breathe, laugh, or move in any way. The amazing multichambered heart that pumps blood around your entire body every few seconds is also a muscle.

Neurons – These cells carry signals that communicate with the entire body, coordinate all internal processes, and help us remember where the car keys are located. They exist throughout the body, but in the brain they come together in a remarkable array that provides a network of 100 trillion connections. There are roughly as many connections in the brain as there are cells in the body. Each neuron is wrapped on the outer surface by a covering that insulates the cell to keep the signals from short-circuiting. This outer wrapping, called myelin, is key to the health of neurons throughout the body.

Though the neurons form a network within the brain, they actually are not physically connected to one another. At a junction point, the electrochemical current that has been carried along the outer membrane of one neuron is translated into a biochemical message which crosses the gap to the next neuron, and is translated back into a signal that can be carried on. This all happens very quickly, in nanotime in fact. The clustering of the neurons in this nonhardwired way allows the brain to change connections, drop connections, or make new connections as needed. This neuroplasticity is a hot topic in brain research today.

Glial cells – Once thought to be nothing more than a scaffoldlike structure for brain neurons to grow or rest on, the white matter of the brain is now recognized as yet another transmitting network. In contrast to the neuron-rich gray matter, astrocytes—one type of glial cell—connect physically to one another and do not communicate via electrochemical transmission. Though less is known about the role and function of glia, there are ten times more of these cell structures in the brain than there are neurons.

Connective Tissue – Tendons and cartilage provide the attachment points for the bones and appendages such as the ears and nose. It also allows for smooth joint function. This tissue is less rich in blood supply, and though it heals more slowly, it does have its own healing mechanisms. Fibroblasts are the key cells responsible for the repair of connective tissue.

Intestines – The intestines are lined with cells that have tiny fingerlike projections called microvilli. These projections allow for maximum surface area to draw out the nutrients from the food we eat. Should the microvilli be disrupted, less absorption takes place, and it is difficult—or impossible—for the body to be properly nourished. Gut cells have special zipperlike connections between them so that they can stretch without bursting.

Nerves – Yes, we saw them previously in the brain, but they run throughout the body as well carrying impulses back and forth. Nerve cells in the body are some of the longest we have. Like the ones in the brain these cells are also wrapped in myelin to insulate the impulses being carried. Nerves carry impulses to muscles and provide our sense of touch, including sensations of pressure and pain. We have more nerves cells in our faces than anywhere else, with the highest concentration in the tongue. That's why we are so good at finding the cherry pit in that piece of pie, before we chomp down on it. A hair in your food—ew, but yes, the tongue found it before you swallowed. Having that sensitivity keeps us safe.

Blood – Two main types of cells—red and white—circulate throughout the body. Red blood cells carry oxygen and remove carbon dioxide. This cell type has no nucleus and therefore does not divide the way cells do. That's a good thing, as spontaneous increases in blood volume due to cell division could be problematic for the body. These cells typically live for about four months and are then cleaned up by the spleen and recycled. New red blood cells are created in the bone marrow, predominantly in the head of the femur, and are released into the blood stream at the approximate rate of 3 million per second. One red blood cell can make a full circuit from the heart and back in 20 seconds.

White cells in our blood fight off infection. In response to inflammation they travel to sites in the body where they are needed. That's the good thing about inflammation, it is a communication device—a call for help—but over the long term inflammation can be injurious to tissues and can exhaust the immune system.

Liver – The cells in the liver are responsible for cleaning up toxins in the blood, and producing a number of metabolic compounds. The largest internal organ, its size speaks to how important it is in keeping us alive and well. Cells within the liver have several different ways of protecting us from harmful substances. These cells can alter, recycle, or sequester toxins, viruses, and other agents of disease. Whatever enters the body in some way will pass through, touch, and be touched by liver cells.

Kidneys – The metabolic by-products of our lives as humans contains uric acid and urea, both of which must be released systematically by the body. The kidneys constantly filter urea and uric acid from our blood. Without the cleansing work of the kidneys we can experience pain in the joints from crystallized uric acid and a host of other diseases.

Pancreas – The cells in the pancreas produce various hormones and enzymes that are key to our digestion and metabolism. This dual function means this organ is considered to be both a part of the endocrine and exocrine systems in the body. Within the organ there are endocrine cells called the islets of Langerhans—one of the coolest names in science—that produce insulin and other hormones that are distributed throughout the body via the bloodstream. The exocrine function is provided by the acini cells, which make digestive enzymes that pass directly into the small intestine via a system of ducts.

Skin – These cells are part of the largest organ of the body. Layers and layers of skin cells of various types provide protection from external forces. Under magnification, the outermost layers, made up of dead cells, look like piles of old paper. Skin is highly elastic, and fairly waterproof, and it provides for temperature control and elimination of certain waste products.

Fat – Fat cells are packets of stored fuel, which the body can use as needed and which provide insulation from cold. A certain reserve of these cells can be beneficial when the body is experiencing illness or deprivation, but too much fat is problematic, causing extra stress on the cardiovascular system, skeletal structure, and altering hormone balance. There is some evidence that excess fat causes a degree of inflammation, which in turn may overburden the immune system.

The body microcosm matches at the cellular level the activities we pursue in the outer world. As humans we are repositories of information and personal experience, we need and use power, we act and produce things, and we communicate with one another. The quality of our outer life resonates in our cells, and the vibrancy within us is mirrored in our daily life.

ACKNOWLEDGMENTS

A book is the work of many hands, all of them important and some crucial. To all of these pivotal people I offer my thanks.

To Helen Folsom for her sustained support and quintessential editorial skills.

To the Hay House team. You are wonderfully astute and a delight to work with.

To my daughter and son-in-law who remind me what is important in life.

To clients, readers, and students whose questions inspired and informed me. When you asked "Is the new book done?" you kept me on track.

To friends and colleagues who tolerated the creative process with kindness and humor.

To Teresa Barker for her editorial assistance, particularly with the proposal.

To my agent, Stephanie Tade. Your encouragement, wise advise, and clarity has made this project better at every turn.

ENDNOTES

Introduction

1. P. M. Barnes, et al., *Complementary and Alternative Medicine Use Among Adults and Children: United States 2007*, CDC National Health Statistics, Report #12, 2008.

Chapter 1: Appreciation and Awareness

1. Sharon Begley, "Can You Build a Better Brain?" *Newsweek,* January 10, 2011, 41–45.

2. Carl Zimmer, "100 Trillion Connections," *Scientific American,* January 2011, 59–63

3. Miller, Kenneth D., "π=Visual Cortex," *Science* 330 (2010):1059–1060.

4. Richard J. Davidson, et al., "Alterations in Brain and Immune Function Produced by Mindfulness Meditation," *Psychosomatic Medicine* 65, no. 4 (2003): 564–570.

5. Rollin McCraty, Ph.D. and Doc Childre, *The Appreciative Heart: The Psychophysiology of Positive Emotions and Optimal Functioning* (Boulder Creek, CA: Institute of HeartMath, 2002).

6. R. Emmons, et al., *Handbook of Positive Psychology Assessment* (Washington, DC: American Psychological Association, 2003).

7.   Alice M. Isen, "An Influence of Positive Affect on Decision Making in Complex Situations," *Journal of Consumer Psychology* 11, no. 2 (2001):75–85.

8.   Ibid.

Chapter 2: Intuition and Action

1.   David G. Myers, *Intuition: Its Powers and Perils* (New Haven, CT: Yale University Press, 2002).

2.   Richard H. Thaler and Cass R. Sunstein, *Nudge: Improving Decisions About Health, Wealth, and Happiness* (New Haven, CT: Yale University Press, 2008).

3.   Larry Dossey, *Reinventing Medicine: Beyond Mind–Body to a New Era of Healing* (San Francisco: Harper San Francisco, 2000).

4.   Silvia P. Westphal, "High Hopes for a New Kind of Gene," *Smithsonian*, July 2009, 72–79.

5.   Dean Radin, *Entangled Minds: Extrasensory Experiences in a Quantum Reality* (New York: Paraview Pocket Books, 2006).

Chapter 3: Presence and Communication

1.   L. Bryan Ray, et al., "An Insider's View," *Science* 318 (2007):5847.

2.   Stephen J. Simpson, "Intercellular Traffic," *Science* 305 (2004):5687.

3.   L. Bryan Ray, "A Message in a Vesicle," *Science* 326 (2009):1590.

4.   Rudolf Otto, *The Idea of the Holy: An Inquiry into the Non-Rational Factor in the Idea of the Divine and Its Relation to the Rational,* trans. John W. Harvey (London: Oxford University Press, 1971).

5.   Richard Katz, *Boiling Energy: Community Healing Among the Kalahari Kung* (Cambridge, MA: Harvard University Press, 1982).

Chapter 4: Connection and Protection

1.   Joyce W. Hawkes, *Cell-Level Healing: The Bridge from Soul to Cell* (Portland, OR: Beyond Words, 2006).

2.   Benoit Kornmann, et al., "An ER-Mitochondria Tethering Complex Revealed by a Synthetic Biology Screen," *Science* 325 (2009):477–481.

Chapter 5: Balance and Harmony

1.   "By the Numbers: The Body Game," *Scientific American Illustrated*, November–December 2010, 72.

2.   Ibid., 73.

3.   Bruce Alberts, et al., *The Molecular Biology of the Cell* (New York: Garland Science, 2002), pp. 1010–1011.

4.   Roberto Bonasio, et al., "Molecular Signals of Epigenetic States," *Science* 330 (2010):612–616.

5.   Guy Riddihough and Laura M. Zahn, "What Is Epigenetics?" *Science* 330 (2010):611.

6.   Greg Miller, "The Seductive Allure of Behavioral Epigenetics," *Science* 329 (2010):24–27.

Chapter 6: Compassion and Clarity

1.   C. Kerr, et al., "Cortical Dynamics as a Therapeutic Mechanism for Touch Healing," *Journal of Alternative and Complementary Medicine* 13 (2007):59–66. Also S. Lazar, et al., "Meditation Experience Is Associated with Increased Cortical Thickness," *NeuroReport* 16 (2005):1893.

2.   John Hick, *Evil and the God of Love* (San Francisco: Harper San Francisco, 1978).

3.   Kent A. Kiehl and Joshua W. Buckholtz, "Inside the Mind of a Psychopath," *Scientific American,* September–October 2010, 22–29.

4. Stephen Hawking and Leonard Mlodinow, "The Elusive Theory of Everything," *Scientific American*, September 2010, 68–71.

5. Stephen Hawking and Leonard Mlodinow, *The Grand Design* (New York: Bantam, 2010), 46.

Chapter 7: Attention and Focus

1. J. W. Hawkes, "The Effects of Laser Irradiation on Fish Chromatophores," *Pigment Cell* 3 (1976):345–356.

Chapter 8: Sensitivity and Joy

1. Jadzia Jagiellowicz, et al., "The Trait of Sensory Processing Sensitivity and Neural Responses to Changes in Visual Scenes," *Social Cognitive and Affective Neuroscience Advance Access,* March 4, 2010: scan.oxfordjournals.org/content/early/2010/03/04/scan.nsq001.full.

2. Laura Spinney, "You Smell Flowers, I Smell Stale Urine," *Scientific American,* February 2011, 26.

3. Oliver Sacks, *The Mind's Eye* (New York: Alfred A. Knopf, 2010).

4. Richard Russell, et al., "Super-Recognizers: People with Extraordinary Face Recognition Ability," *Psychonomic Bulletin and Review* 16, no. 2 (2009):252–257.

Appendix: A Simple Guide to Cell Biology

1. Melinda W. Moyer, "The Importance of Junk DNA," *Scientific American,* December 2010, 53.

RESOURCES

Braden, Gregg. 2008. *The Divine Matrix: Bridging Time, Space, Miracles, and Belief.* Hay House.

Dispenza, Joe. 2008. *Evolve Your Brain: The Science of Changing Your Mind.* HCI.

Elias, Jack. 2005. *Finding True Magic: Transpersonal Hypnosis and Hypnotherapy/NLP.* Five Wisdoms Press.

McTaggart, Lynne. 2011. *The Bond: Connecting Through the Space Between Us.* Free Press.

Oz, Mehmet, and Michael F. Roizen. 2008. *YOU: The Owner's Manual, Updated and expanded Edition: An Insider's Guide to the Body that Will Make You Healthier and Younger.* William Morrow.

Pert, Candace. 1999. *Molecules Of Emotion: The Science Behind Mind-Body Medicine.* Simon & Schuster.

Schwartz, Ph.D. 2011. *The Sacred Promise: How Science Is Discovering Spirit's Collaboration with Us in Our Daily Lives.* Atria Books/Beyond Words.

Targ, Russell, and Jane Katra, Ph.D. 1999. *Miracles of Mind: Exploring Nonlocal Consciousness and Spiritual Healing.* New World Library.

www.eomega.org, Omega Institute for Holistic Studies, Rhinebeck, NY.

www.iands.org, International Association for Near-Death Studies, Durham, NC.

www.iiihs.org/iiihs.html, International Institute of Integral Human Sciences, Montreal, Canada.

www.raganiworld.com, Kirtan with Ragani. My favorite album: *Best of Both Worlds.*

INDEX

ABOUT THE AUTHOR

Joyce Hawkes's work has spanned nearly 40 years, half of them in solid scientific research in cellular biology, and half in healing practices, many of them grounded in indigenous healing traditions. She spent 20 years researching the extraordinary resiliency of cells under siege from environmental pollutants. As a postdoctoral Fellow with the National Institutes of Health, a supervisory research biologist for the National Marine Fisheries Service (a division of NOAA), she published scholarly research. In scientific conferences as a presenter, Joyce conversed and collaborated with distinguished colleagues from all over the world before she discovered the phenomenon she calls cell-level healing and resonance. As a graduate student and later in the work of completing her doctorate as a cell biologist and biophysicist, she studied cells using the most sophisticated tool in existence for that purpose: the electron microscope. The electron microscope, invented in about 1945, weighs one ton, works on 100,000 volts of electricity, and has the capacity to magnify the inner life of the cell up to one million times. At that magnification, secrets of cells have emerged that had eluded scientists for centuries. She spent her workdays on that exciting frontier of scientific exploration. Joyce's research was honored by election to the American Association for the Advancement of Science as a Fellow, a position she currently maintains.

Her life took a surprising twist after a near-death experience triggered by a fluke accident at home. She recovered quickly, but soon found herself drawn in a different way to the study of cells and the internal mechanisms for healing. Increasingly attuned to the healing power of mind, body, and spirit in concert, eventually she left the formal laboratory with its advanced instruments to study health and healing with indigenous healers around the globe, from tropical forests to black-sand beaches—the most low-tech settings imaginable. In the midst of these travels and studies, Joyce also completed a Master's degree in Pastoral Ministry at Seattle University, a Jesuit school, and served as an intern with the First Baptist Church of Seattle. The broad range of studies and subsequent deep understanding of Western and Eastern theology and healing traditions has supported her personal journey and has helped her be open and welcoming to all people.

She sought ways to use the natural synergy between cells and consciousness to enrich everyday health and help repair the body when injured or ill. Joyce's twin passions for studying both science and spirit drew her into this expanded field of exploration and practice. These extraordinary opportunities—particularly with indigenous healers in the vast world of non-Western practices such as Bali, the hinterlands of the Philippines, southern India, and Tibetan Buddhists down the street in Seattle—opened an experience of new dimensions of spiritual and healing practices and opened her mind to the powerful effects of healing states of mind. In these cultures, attention to spiritual practice is not called upon solely in times of illness, but daily to maintain vitality, keep the body renewed, and to support robust health in the dimensions of body, mind, and spirit.

In addition, the combination of science and work with non-Western healers opened a rather unique path that Joyce applies to writing, teaching, and to her keynote presentations at conferences. This is a particularly rich time to share the wisdom of these experiences and relate them to practices that support health, as evidenced by continued invitations to speak and teach workshops. Along with a busy speaking and teaching travel schedule, Joyce's private practice is busy. Her clients live all over the world and she works with them in person in her Seattle office, by telephone, and by Skype with those in England, Australia, Canada, Poland, and across the United States.

She can be reached at: www.celllevelhealing.com.

NOTES

NOTES

NOTES

NOTES

NOTES

NOTES

NOTES

NOTES